THE QUILTER'S RECIPE BOOK

All the ingredients
you need to
create over
100 fabulous quilts

CELIA EDDY

BARRON'S

A QUARTO BOOK

Copyright © 2005 Quarto Inc.

First edition for the United States, its territories and dependencies, and Canada published in 2005 by Barron's Educational Series, Inc.

All inquiries should be addressed to:
Barron's Educational Series, Inc.
250 Wireless Boulevard
Hauppauge, NY 11788
www.barronseduc.com

Library of Congress Catalog Card Number: 2003116939

International Standard Book Number: 0-7641-2955-4

Conceived, designed, and produced by
Quarto Publishing plc
The Old Brewery
6 Blundell Street
London N7 9BH

QUAR: QBI

Editor Michelle Pickering
Art editor & designer
  Julie Francis
Illustrators Jennie Dooge,
  Kuo Kang Chen
Photographer Paul Forrester
Indexer Dorothy Frame
Assistant art director
  Penny Cobb

Art director Moira Clinch
Publisher Piers Spence

Color separation by
Provision Pte Ltd, Singapore
Printed by Star Standard
Industries (Pte) Ltd, Singapore

9 8 7 6 5 4 3 2 1

Contents

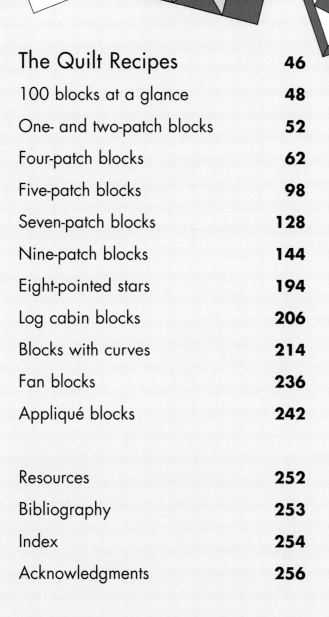

Introduction

Quilt making, like cooking, offers something for everyone—and anyone can do it. After all, making a quilt is a bit like baking a cake. First you need a list of all the equipment and ingredients, then you follow the step-by-step recipe instructions for putting everything together.

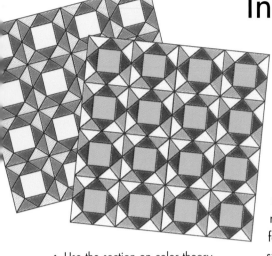

▲ Use the section on color theory and design to help you choose a color scheme for your quilt.

In Chapter 1 you will find an explanation of all the tools, materials, and techniques you need to make a quilt. Chapter 2 features 100 quilt recipes with step-by-step instructions for making them. What could be simpler?

Of course, experienced cooks often bring their own magic touch to a basic recipe by adding extra ingredients or making imaginative adaptations. In this book you will find 100 basic quilt recipes, but as you progress you will see lots of ways to adapt or change them creatively. Some alternative settings and variations are shown for each quilt block, but these are just a few of many possibilities. And remember, quilts do not have to be big. All of the patterns in this book make wonderful wall quilts, chair throws, bags, and even clothes. So choose a recipe and cook up a quilt.

▲ Chapter 1 explains all the basic techniques step by step.

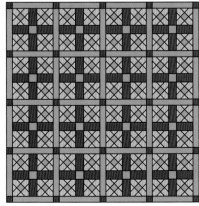

◀ ▲ Each quilt recipe features a photograph of a finished quilt, plus some examples of different settings and color schemes you could use. This quilt, Bachelor's Puzzle, can be found on page 102.

Cooking up a quilt

All 100 quilt blocks are displayed together on pages 48–51. Choose the one you want to make, then turn to the recipe page indicated.

Step 1: Check the skill level to get an idea of how easy or complicated the block is; each block is graded with 1, 2, or 3 sewing machine icons, with 1 icon being the easiest.

Step 2: Each recipe features a photograph of a finished quilt. Underneath you will find some general information and tips about that particular quilt block.

Step 6: Follow the step-by-step instructions for cutting the patches and piecing them together. Each step has an icon for cutting, machine sewing, or hand sewing. The sewing method indicated is only a suggestion; if you prefer to hand sew everything, do so, and vice versa. Refer back to Chapter 1 whenever you need to brush up on the basic techniques.

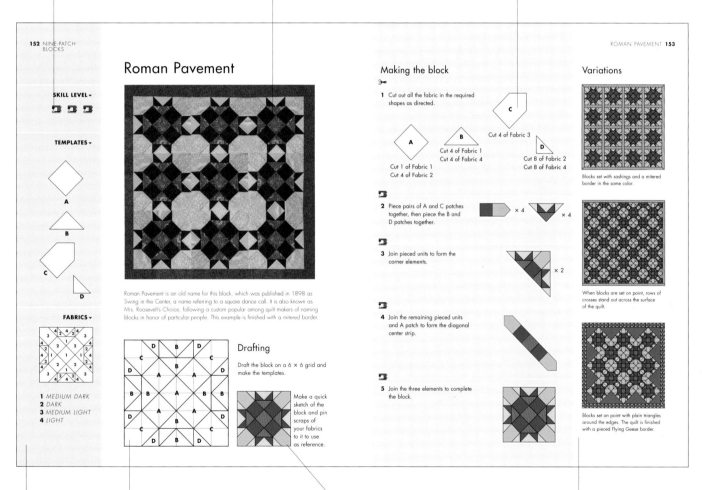

Step 3: Check the "ingredients" column to see what templates and fabrics you will need for each block.

Step 4: Draft or enlarge the block diagram on which the quilt is based and make the templates. If you use a photocopier to do this, enlarging the diagram by 464 percent will create an approximately 12-inch (30-cm) block. If the photocopier will not enlarge by this much, start by enlarging the diagram by 232 percent, then enlarge the enlargement by 200 percent.

Step 5: Make a quick sketch of your block and pin scraps of your chosen fabrics to it to double-check that you are happy with your choices and to use as reference when making the block. That's all the preparation; now it's time to start cooking.

Step 7: Decide how you want to lay out the finished blocks in the quilt. Some variations are given for each block, but these are only suggestions, and there are many other possibilities. Look back at Chapter 1 for ideas for quilting designs.

Tools, Materials, and Techniques

This chapter outlines all the equipment and materials you will need, plus the basic techniques for making a quilt, from drafting principles and sewing techniques to quilting designs and finishing methods. If you are new to quilt making, practice on scrap fabric before embarking on a quilt. If you have made a quilt before, use this chapter as reference whenever you need to.

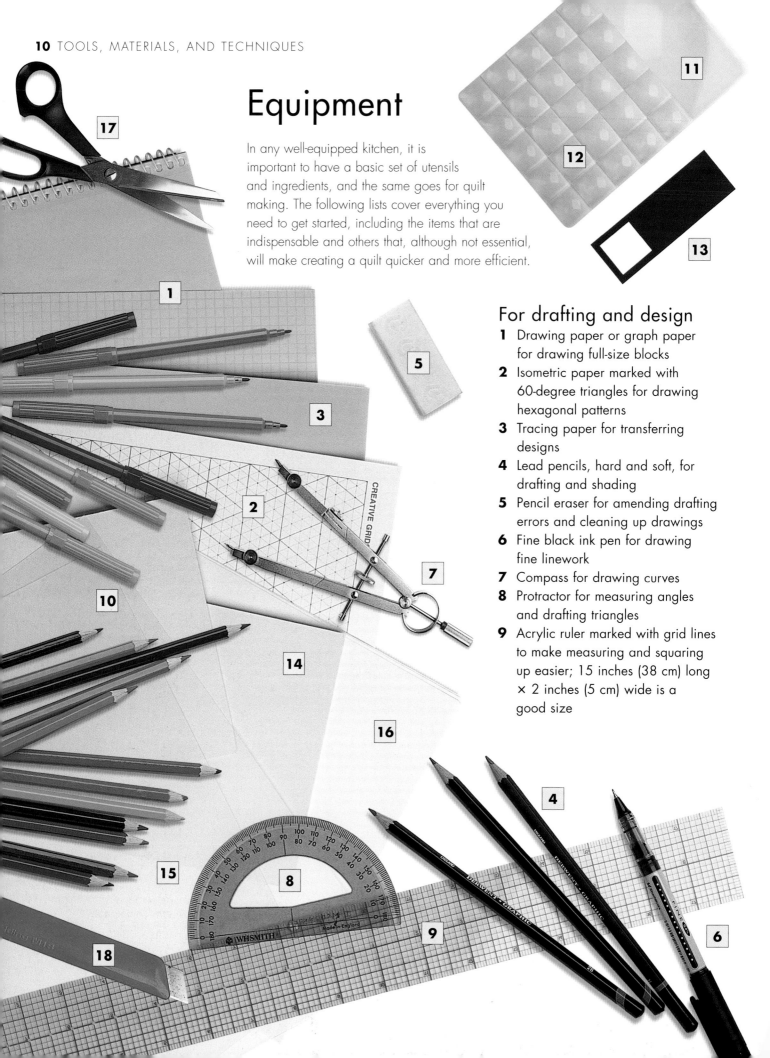

Equipment

In any well-equipped kitchen, it is important to have a basic set of utensils and ingredients, and the same goes for quilt making. The following lists cover everything you need to get started, including the items that are indispensable and others that, although not essential, will make creating a quilt quicker and more efficient.

For drafting and design

1 Drawing paper or graph paper for drawing full-size blocks

2 Isometric paper marked with 60-degree triangles for drawing hexagonal patterns

3 Tracing paper for transferring designs

4 Lead pencils, hard and soft, for drafting and shading

5 Pencil eraser for amending drafting errors and cleaning up drawings

6 Fine black ink pen for drawing fine linework

7 Compass for drawing curves

8 Protractor for measuring angles and drafting triangles

9 Acrylic ruler marked with grid lines to make measuring and squaring up easier; 15 inches (38 cm) long × 2 inches (5 cm) wide is a good size

For assessing colors

10 Good-quality colored or fiber-tipped pens for experimenting with different color designs

11 Reducing glass—shows how fabrics will look from a distance (you can get the same effect by looking through the wrong end of a pair of binoculars)

12 Multi-image lens—a Perspex (acrylic) sheet, through which you can see how one block will look when multiplied

13 Value finder—a red or green lens that eliminates color but reveals the relative dark/light tonal value of the fabrics (the red lens is not effective with red fabrics; the green lens is not effective with green fabrics)

For making templates

14 Cardboard for making templates

15 Template plastic for making transparent templates

16 Heavy quality paper for English patchwork

17 Paper scissors for cutting out paper, cardboard, and plastic

18 Craft knife for cutting out cardboard pieces

19 Metal ruler for use with craft knife

For cutting fabric

20 Large fabric scissors; those with spring-loaded handles are easier to use if you have hand or wrist problems

21 Rotary cutter to speed up the cutting process when cutting lots of patches and strips, and trimming finished blocks; there are many different sizes, but the most commonly used has a 1¼-inch (3-cm) diameter blade

22 Self-healing mat for use with a rotary cutter; a 17 × 23-inch (43 × 58-cm) mat is ideal for general purposes

23 A 6 × 24-inch (15 × 60-cm) acrylic ruler for use with rotary cutter and mat

24 A 12 × 12-inch (30 × 30-cm) acrylic square for cutting squares of all sizes and for squaring up blocks

25 Special-purpose acrylic rulers for cutting triangles, curves, and so on

COMPUTER-AIDED DESIGN

Some dedicated quilting programs are available that allow you to design quilts and arrange sizes and layouts. In some programs, the quantities of fabric required for a particular project can be calculated and templates of the required size can be printed out. You can also use general computer graphics programs for designing quilts.

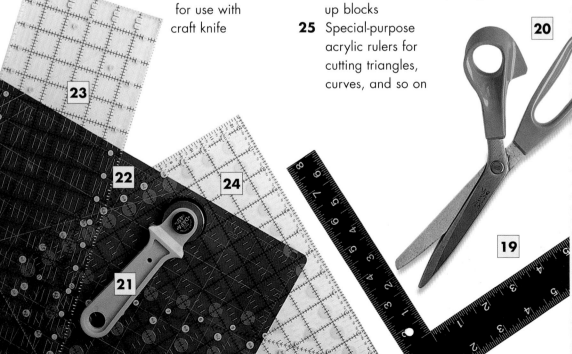

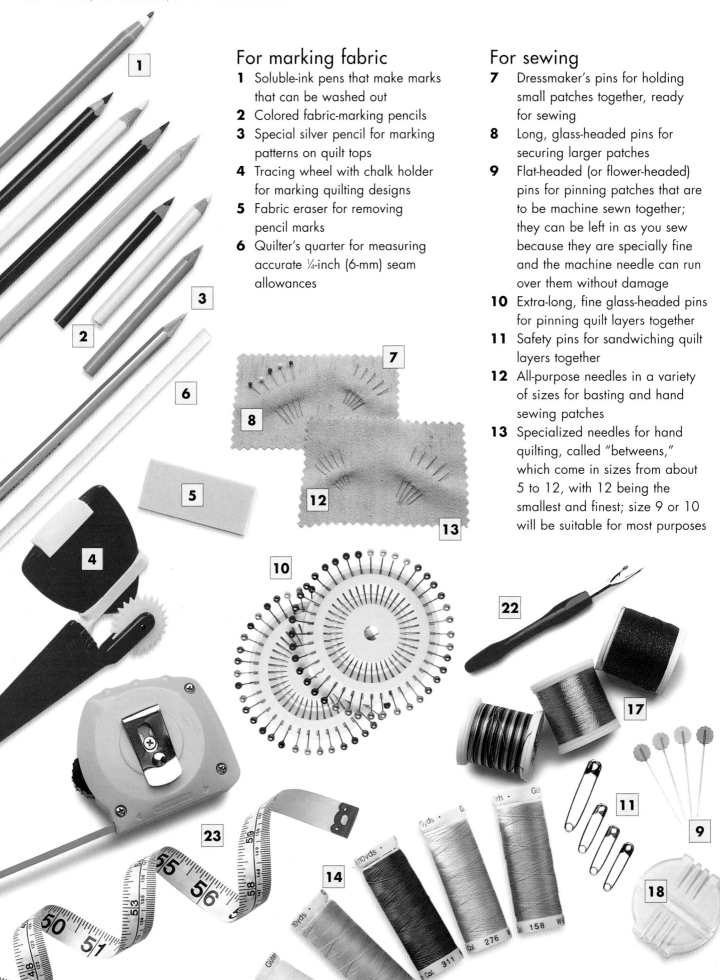

For marking fabric

1 Soluble-ink pens that make marks that can be washed out

2 Colored fabric-marking pencils

3 Special silver pencil for marking patterns on quilt tops

4 Tracing wheel with chalk holder for marking quilting designs

5 Fabric eraser for removing pencil marks

6 Quilter's quarter for measuring accurate ¼-inch (6-mm) seam allowances

For sewing

7 Dressmaker's pins for holding small patches together, ready for sewing

8 Long, glass-headed pins for securing larger patches

9 Flat-headed (or flower-headed) pins for pinning patches that are to be machine sewn together; they can be left in as you sew because they are specially fine and the machine needle can run over them without damage

10 Extra-long, fine glass-headed pins for pinning quilt layers together

11 Safety pins for sandwiching quilt layers together

12 All-purpose needles in a variety of sizes for basting and hand sewing patches

13 Specialized needles for hand quilting, called "betweens," which come in sizes from about 5 to 12, with 12 being the smallest and finest; size 9 or 10 will be suitable for most purposes

14 Good-quality machine sewing threads

15 Quilting threads for hand quilting

16 Basting thread

17 Embroidery and metallic threads for embellishment

18 Beeswax to prevent thread from knotting and to strengthen it when hand stitching

19 Metal thimble for sewing; thimbles with flattened crowns are good for hand quilting

20 Finger guard (usually made of leather) for protecting the finger that is held underneath the quilt when hand quilting

21 Small, sharp scissors for snipping machine threads and trimming corners; use them for small jobs to save your large fabric-cutting scissors from becoming blunt

22 Seam ripper for unpicking stitches without damaging the fabric and for any job requiring a small, sharp point, such as holding down small patches while you are using a sewing machine

23 Tape measure for measuring blocks, sashings, and so on; a metal tape measure is more accurate for large items such as finished quilts

24 Hoops and frames in different sizes for holding the quilt for quilting; a floor frame will hold large quilts without the need for basting the layers together, if you have the space for it

25 Fusible webbing that has adhesive on one side and paper on the other for holding appliqué patches in place, ready for sewing

Sewing machine

Unless you are a dedicated hand stitcher, you will probably regard your sewing machine as your best friend. Treat it well by following the manufacturer's maintenance instructions and get it serviced regularly. Useful features for a quilter are a zigzag stitch and a reverse-stitch function, which enables you to secure seams at start and finish. Useful accessories include a straight-stitch foot plate (with a round hole to prevent the needle from straying off line) and a foot with a ¼-inch (6-mm) guide to help keep an accurate seam allowance when sewing patches. A walking or even-feed foot, a darning foot, and a means of covering or dropping the feed dogs are useful for machine quilting.

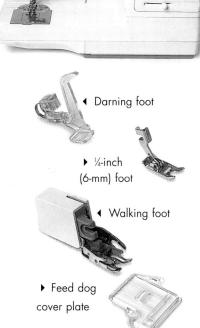

◄ Darning foot

► ¼-inch (6-mm) foot

◄ Walking foot

► Feed dog cover plate

Materials

The obvious material you need for quilting is, of course, fabric, and there are some practical considerations to keep in mind. The first thing to consider is the purpose of the finished quilt. An item such as a bed quilt should be made from hard-wearing and fully washable fabrics. A purely decorative item such as a wall hanging, however, can be made from almost any type of fabric.

▲ Pure cotton fabrics are ideal for making quilts and come in a wide range of colors and patterns.

Types of fabric

The most useful type of fabric for patchwork is pure cotton. Cotton is washable and holds its shape well, and it is easy to stitch through several layers when quilting. It is also available in the widest range of colors and patterns. Cotton/polyester blends can also be used, but they are more slippery to sew and tend to be more transparent than pure cotton. Many synthetic fabrics are too slippery and loosely woven for quilting, but firm varieties such as polyester silk can be sewn successfully.

Exotic fabrics such as silk, satin, velvet, and taffeta provide richness, sheen, and texture to a quilt, and some types can be washed. These fabrics are usually more difficult to handle than cotton. Fine silks, for example, can be very slippery, but you can make them easier to sew by ironing them onto a lightweight fusible webbing before cutting them out. Avoid using thick fabrics when sewing small patches because they are less flexible and therefore harder to sew than thinner fabrics.

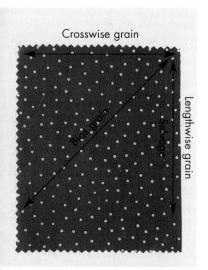

Crosswise grain

Bias grain

Selvage

Lengthwise grain

FABRIC GRAIN

It is important to recognize the grain of the fabric when cutting out patches. Fabrics are made by weaving lengthwise and crosswise fibers together. The lengthwise grain runs parallel to the selvage (the finished edge). The crosswise grain runs perpendicular to this. A bias grain runs diagonally across the fabric.

▲ Cotton/polyester blends can be used but may be a little slippery to sew.

▼ Using exotic fabrics such as silk, brocade, damask, and velvet can give your quilt wonderful depth and sheen.

Other materials

In addition to the fabric for the blocks, you will need lining or backing fabric for the finished quilt. You can use patchwork cotton or other, cheaper cotton fabrics such as curtain lining. If you want to hand quilt, avoid thick or densely textured backing fabrics.

Batting (also known as wadding) goes between the top of the quilt and the backing. Some battings need closer quilting than others, so read the manufacturer's information to find out how much or how little quilting is required. The main types of batting are polyester, cotton, wool, and silk. Polyester is available in different weights. Buy only good-quality polyester batting, because cheaper versions may cause "bearding"—that is, the fibers migrate through the top layer and appear as a fine mist on the quilt surface. Needle-punched polyester is firm and dense and usually will not beard. There are many cotton versions on the market, including some that are mixtures of cotton and man-made fibers. Wool batting is very soft and easily quilted, and silk is beautifully soft and easy to quilt.

▲ Choose a backing fabric that complements the colors in the front of the quilt.

◀ There are many different types of batting, including polyester, cotton, and wool.

Fabric quantities

It is not difficult to estimate quantities for making a small item, but if you are planning a large quilt for which you need to buy fabrics, it is important to know how much will be needed before you start sewing. Make the templates for your block, cut out patches in either paper or scrap fabrics, then place them as economically as possible on fabric that is the width of the fabric you intend to buy. If you do this for each fabric you will be using in the block and add a generous allowance of at least 10 percent to be safe, that will give you an idea of how much to buy. Alternatively, make a single block and multiply the quantity of each fabric used by the number of blocks you want to make.

For batting and lining, measure width by length to get the size of the pieces needed, then add at least 2 inches (5 cm) all around because there will be some shrinkage during quilting.

▼ Place paper patches on the fabric to help you calculate the quantity of fabric required.

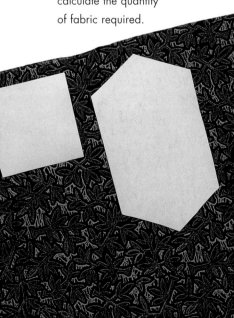

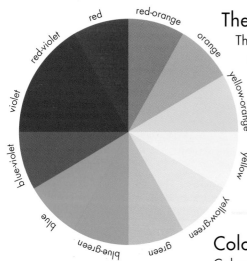

▲ Dogstooth Violet (page 78) in primary colors on a neutral ground.

Choosing Colors

One of the most fundamental skills involved in creating a successful quilt is the use of color. Some people seem to have more of an aptitude for color than others, but it is possible to learn how to use it to great effect by exploring the basic principles of color theory. Always remember, however, that color is a personal choice and that there are no hard-and-fast rules.

The color wheel

The relationship between different colors can be demonstrated on a color wheel showing the primary, secondary, and tertiary colors. The primary colors are red, yellow, and blue. Secondary colors are made by mixing two primary colors together, producing orange, green, and violet. Tertiary colors are produced by mixing a primary color with the secondary color nearest to it on the wheel: red-orange, yellow-orange, yellow-green, blue-green, blue-violet, and red-violet.

Color qualities

Colors that are opposite each other on the color wheel are said to be complementary—red and green or blue and yellow, for example. They create vibrancy when placed next to each other. Colors that are close to each other on the color wheel, such as violet and blue or yellow and green, are said to be analogous and produce a more subtle and harmonious effect when combined. Adding a small amount of a complementary color to analogous colors will provide sparkle—adding a touch of yellow to blues and violets, for example.

Combining a color with colors that are midway around the color wheel, such as red with blue or yellow-green with blue-green, is known as a contrasting or clashing color scheme. This creates a discordant effect that can be dramatic but needs to be used with care. Separating clashing colors with a third color can solve the problem—separating yellow-green and blue-green with orange, for instance.

▲ Complementary colors such as red and green are opposite each other on the color wheel.

▼ Clashing colors such as turquoise and lime green can be successful if separated by a third color such as orange.

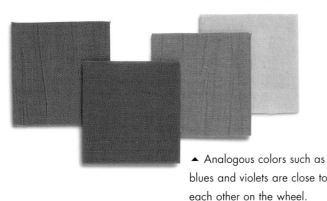

▲ Analogous colors such as blues and violets are close to each other on the wheel.

Tonal value and color temperature

Other characteristics to keep in mind when choosing colors are whether their tonal value is light or dark. The placement of light and dark fabrics in a block can dramatically enhance the pieced pattern. Another factor is whether colors are warm or cool. Reds, browns, pinks, and purples are generally warm colors, whereas blues and greens are cool. Combining warm/cool and light/dark colors can create useful optical illusions, with warm/light colors appearing to advance and cool/dark colors appearing to recede. Use this knowledge to help set a mood or style for a quilt.

▶ Warm colors such as pink appear to advance, whereas cool colors such as green recede.

▲ All colors come in a range of tonal values from dark to light.

Neutrals

Neutral colors, such as white, black, cream, brown, and gray, do not appear as pure colors on the color wheel but are made by mixing pure colors together. For example, if an artist mixed pigments of all three primaries together in equal intensities, the result would be black. Mixing pigments of colors opposite each other on the color wheel produces a range of grays and browns. Neutrals, therefore, work well with all colors on the color wheel and can be used to great effect in patchwork, especially in backgrounds and to set off other colors.

▲ Neutrals such as gray, brown, cream, white, and black work well with all colors on the color wheel.

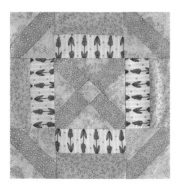

▲ Girl's Joy (page 136) in light tonal values.

▲ Hue

▲ Tonal value

▲ Intensity

COLOR TERMINOLOGY

HUE is the actual color on the wheel: red, blue, and green, for example.

TONAL VALUE describes the lightness or darkness of the color on a scale from white to black.

INTENSITY describes the depth, saturation, and impact of the color.

Designing with Fabric

The next stage is to put your color theory into practice by choosing fabrics that will enhance the design of the block you wish to make. Patchwork fabrics are often produced in color-coordinated ranges that include solids, large and small prints, checks, stripes, and so on. If you want to give your quilt a coherent look, these fabrics can be a wonderful aid, and you can always supplement the range by adding some fabrics of your own choice.

Solids and patterns

Quilt makers have a wide variety of fabrics to choose from. Blocks can look striking when pieced entirely from solid fabrics, but take care that they do not become too stark. Patterns, such as stripes and checks, offer many design possibilities, and by careful placement, the simplest block can have an interesting visual effect.

Fabrics with small all-over prints are ideal for adding texture to a quilt without being too distracting.

Medium and large prints can have a dramatic effect, and fabrics with large motifs are often used in center squares as a feature fabric. There are also plenty of novelty fabrics available that are ideal for center squares and corner posts.

▲ Most quilt fabric suppliers produce coordinated ranges of colors and patterns.

▼ Solid colors are often used to offset patterned fabrics, but they can also make striking quilts on their own.

▼ Novelty fabrics are popular for children's quilts.

▲ Small, medium, and large patterns add multiple colors and visual textures to a quilt.

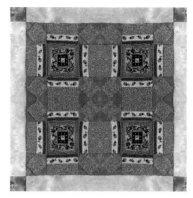

Fussy cutting

Quilters often isolate a picture or motif within a patterned fabric to use for particular patches in a block, such as a center square. Cutting patches in this way is known as fussy cutting or fancy cutting. Use a transparent or window template to isolate the part of the design you wish to use as a feature. Another fussy cutting technique involves choosing particular elements in a patterned fabric to create another pattern. To see what it will look like and figure out how to cut the patches, place a transparent template over the pattern element you want to use, then position two mirrors around it to repeat the element and create a kaleidoscopic effect. Adjust the pieces until you get the result you require, then mark and cut the fabric.

▲ Fussy cutting using a window template.

▲ Fussy cutting using mirrors.

▲ The center squares of these Seven-patch Mosaic blocks (page 132) were fussy cut from striped fabric using mirrors.

Borders and sashings

You need to choose the fabrics for borders and sashings just as carefully as you select the fabrics for the quilt top. Remember that colors are affected by those surrounding them. For example, put a blue border around a scrap quilt comprising many colors and the blues will stand out. Similarly, add a green border and the greens will appear dominant.

▲ The border and posts are in the same fabrics as the internal sashings and posts of the Bear's Paw blocks (page 128).

Trial and error

In any pieced block, the variations you can create by changing and rearranging colors and tones are almost infinite. It is useful at this stage to make a quick sketch of your block and photocopy it several times. Use colored pencils or fiber-tipped pens to try out different color schemes.

When you are happy with a color scheme, try it out with actual fabrics. Make a sketch of your block on a piece of mat board and spray it with temporary adhesive. Snip pieces of fabric and stick them to the board, changing and rearranging them until you are happy with your choices. This will give you a good idea of the visual effect of different combinations before you make a final decision. You can get a good understanding of how the fabrics will look at a distance by looking at them through the wrong end of a pair of binoculars.

▼ Make sketches or use a computer program to try out different color schemes.

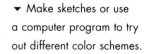

Drafting geometric blocks

First, decide what size your finished block will be. The traditional size of a block is 12 × 12 inches (30 × 30 cm), but you can make it any size you like. You can use plain paper to draft your block diagram, but graph paper divided into ⅛-inch or 1-mm divisions will reduce the amount of measuring you have to do and therefore make the task easier. You will also find it best to use a set square and a very fine black ink pen because these will produce more accurate results.

1 Draw an accurate square of the size you want the block to be, then measure carefully and draw the lines for the grid that you want to use—here, a 4 × 4 grid of 3-inch (7.5-cm) squares.

2 Draw in the lines for the block pattern. Identify the various patches in the block and mark them A, B, and so on.

3 Use a craft knife to cut out one example of each patch needed (if you want to keep your block diagram intact, trace or photocopy the patches onto another piece of paper and cut this). Use these paper patches as guides for making templates.

▲ Broken Pinwheel (page 72) is an easy four-patch geometric block that makes an attractive quilt.

ENLARGING WITH A PHOTOCOPIER

If you use a photocopier to enlarge a block diagram, you will find that the more you enlarge it, the thicker the lines become, making it more difficult to achieve accurate templates. This is not a problem with appliqué designs, but pieced patterns require greater accuracy. One solution is to trace the enlarged diagram using a fine black ink pen, making sure that you draw consistently on either the outside or inside of the lines.

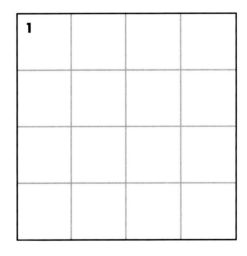

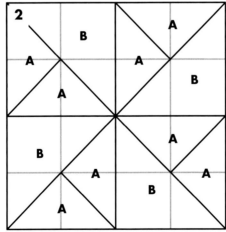

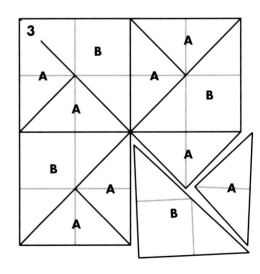

Drafting nongeometric blocks

Some of the patterns in this book include patches with curves and irregular shapes. Smooth curves can be drawn with a compass, but you may find it easier to use a photocopier to enlarge the block diagrams supplied in this book. You can also use the following easy technique to enlarge them.

1 Draw a grid of equal-size squares over the original block diagram (photocopy the diagram if you do not want to mark the book). Use more squares for complicated designs, and fewer squares for easier ones.

2 Draw a square at the size you want the finished block to be, then divide it into the same grid that you have used on the original block diagram. Copy the main lines of the shape onto your enlarged grid, using the squares to help you see where the lines go. Cut out one example of each patch and use these to make templates.

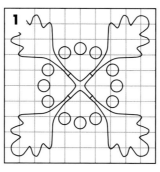

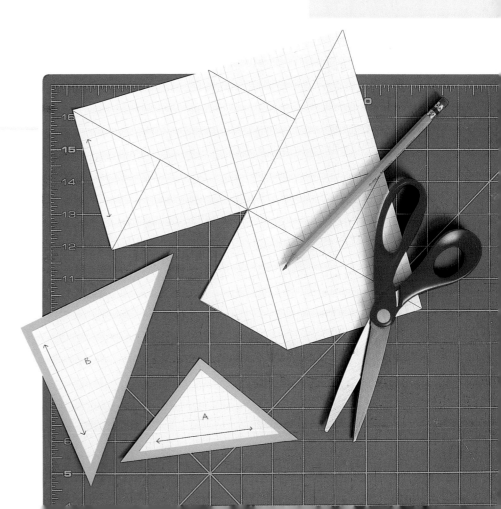

▶ Oak Leaf Wreath (page 246) is a nongeometric block, traditionally made in red and green.

THE RIGHT SIZE

The standard size for blocks is 12 inches (30 cm), but you can use any size you wish. When making a block with lots of small patches, why not draft it up to a larger size? It will make sewing the patches easier and you will need fewer blocks to make your quilt.

Making templates

Glue the patch shapes that you cut from your block diagram onto cardboard or template plastic. Add a ¼-inch (6-mm) seam allowance all around each shape (use a quilter's quarter if you have one) and cut out on the line. Do not add seam allowances if you are making English patchwork and machine appliqué patterns. Use a craft knife if you are using thick cardboard for your templates. Mark the fabric grain line on the templates. This should run vertically and horizontally through the blocks.

Cutting Fabrics

It is important to cut patches accurately so that they fit together properly when you sew them. It is always advisable to wash fabrics before using them, but especially if you are using dark colors that might bleed into lighter fabrics when they are washed. Iron the fabrics well, using spray starch to create a crisp finish. It will make accurate cutting much easier and the fabric will not fray.

Using scissors

Use a sharp pair of fabric scissors and keep them only for cutting fabric. Using them to cut cardboard or paper will blunt them quickly. If you are a beginner, mark and cut one piece of fabric at a time, but increase to several layers as you gain confidence.

1 Lay the templates on the fabric and draw around each shape, using a soft (#2 or 2B) pencil.

2 Cut around each shape on the drawn line, using fabric scissors.

Using a rotary cutter

If you are making a large project, a rotary cutter and self-healing mat make cutting patches a lot quicker and easier. They allow you to cut many different shapes and to cut up to eight layers at a time. Learning to cut accurately takes practice, so try your skills on scrap fabric first. Reverse the instructions if you are left-handed.

SAFETY TIPS

The blade of a rotary cutter is extremely sharp, so take great care when using one. All cutters have a lock that you should engage at the end of each cut. If possible, buy a cutter with an automatic lock that retracts the blade as soon as you stop cutting. When cutting, always run the blade away from you, never toward you. Finally, keep the cutter in a safe place, well away from children.

1 Fold and iron the fabric with selvages together, then place the fabric on the cutting mat with the fold toward you. You need to trim off a strip so that you have a straight edge from which to start cutting. To do this, align a small acrylic square with the folded edge, about 1 inch (2.5 cm) in from the edge you are going to cut. Place a long ruler against the left side of the square, matching its horizontal lines with those of the square.

2 Holding the long ruler firmly in place with your left hand, remove the small square and run a rotary cutter along the right side of the ruler. Cut away from you, not toward you. To keep the ruler in position on long cuts, stop the cutter occasionally and move your left hand up the ruler so that it is even with the cutter.

3 Measure the width of the patch and cut strips of fabric to this width by aligning the vertical line on the ruler with the cut edge of the fabric; for example, for a 4-inch (10-cm) strip, place the 4-inch (10-cm) line of the ruler even with the cut edge of the fabric.

4 Lay the template on the strip and draw around it with a pencil, then use the rotary cutter and ruler to cut along these lines. If you are using ready-made acrylic templates, you can cut directly around them using your rotary cutter, but cardboard or other plastic templates can easily be damaged if you do this.

▲ Road to Oklahoma (page 64) is constructed from squares and half-square triangles, both of which are easy to cut with scissors or a rotary cutter.

ROTARY CUTTING WITHOUT TEMPLATES

You can use a rotary cutter and mat to cut patches without going to the trouble of making templates. It is easy to cut regular shapes such as squares and rectangles like this, using the drafted block for the measurements and adding ¼ inch (6 mm) on all sides for seam allowances. To cut half-square triangles, cut the square ⅞ inch (22 mm) larger than the finished short edge of the triangles to allow for seam allowances at the points of the triangles.

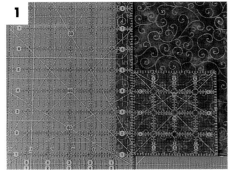
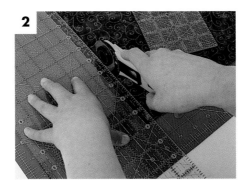
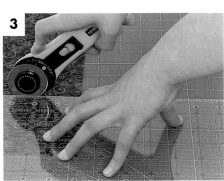

Piecing Techniques

Patchwork can be sewn by hand or by machine. Machine sewing is much faster and therefore particularly useful when working on a sizable project. Sewing by hand is slower, but you can carry your work with you wherever you go and it is easier to make seams meet where they should.

▲ Careful piecing will ensure that the points between blocks align accurately to create interesting subsidiary patterns, such as in this Star Upon Stars quilt (page 202).

▼ Quilter's quarter, pins, and sewing threads—you need very little equipment to sew quilts.

Hand stitching

An accurate seam allowance is important because if it is uneven, the units of the block will not meet up neatly and your blocks may be of uneven sizes. Begin and end each seam exactly ¼ inch (6 mm) from the edge of the fabric; that is, do not sew into the seam allowance. It is a good idea to draw in the stitching line as a guide; you can use a quilter's quarter to do this. Once you have made a few blocks like this, you will probably find that you can estimate the seam allowance accurately just by eye, though you may wish to mark the end of each seam with a small dot or cross to be sure.

1 Place two patches right sides together and pin at regular intervals. Use a fine, sharp needle and thread to match your fabric, or a neutral color if using a variety of fabric colors. Use small, evenly spaced running stitches to sew the seams, making sure that you do not sew into the seam allowance. Take a small backstitch at the beginning and end of each seam for extra strength.

2 When you need to match the seams of two pieced elements, sew to the end of the marked seam, then pass the needle through to the beginning of the next one, without sewing into the allowances of the matching seams. When it comes to pressing the patchwork, the seams can then be pressed in whichever direction you choose. It also avoids having to sew through multiple layers of fabric at once, which can make your fingers sore, particularly if you are sewing lots of patches.

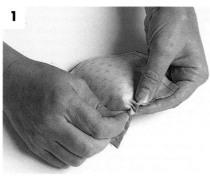

Machine stitching

A straight running stitch is all that is required to join patches and blocks by machine. Check that the tension on your machine is even and set the stitch length to between 9 and 12 stitches per inch (2.5 cm). Lay the patches right sides together with the edges even. Stitch exactly ¼ inch (6 mm) from the edge. You can stitch across the whole length of the seam when machine stitching because sewing through several layers when joining pieced units together is not a problem.

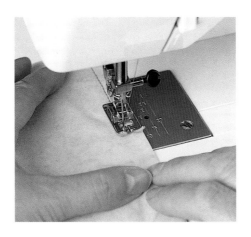

Setting in patches

Most patches can be sewn with straight seams, but some blocks involve awkward angles and the patches have to be "set in" to the angle. The important thing to remember is not to sew into the seam allowance, so it is best to draw in the whole seam lines or mark the ends with a small dot or cross.

1 Place the first two patches right sides together and sew between the marked dots or crosses. At beginning and end, anchor the thread with a small backstitch. Position the third patch.

2 With right sides together, sew the first seam of the third patch exactly to the dot or cross at the awkward angle. Pivot the work so that the final seam lines up, and sew from dot to dot or cross to cross.

3 Gently press the pieced elements with the seam away from the set-in patch, first on the back and then on the front.

1

2

3

1

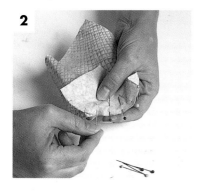

2

3

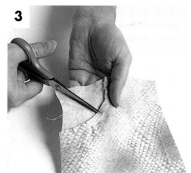

▼ Drunkard's Path (page 214) is constructed entirely from curved patches.

Sewing curves

Curved seams need care but can easily be mastered using the following method.

1 Mark the curves in the drafted pattern at regular intervals; these are known as balance marks. For example, mark the center of the curves and then at regular points between center and edge, using more marks for larger pieces. Transfer the marks on the templates to the fabric patches.

2 Pin the curves at the marked points, then ease the rest of the curves to fit, inserting more pins where necessary.

3 Sew the seam with the concave (inward) curved piece on top, easing the pieces to fit. When finished, snip tiny notches in the convex (outward) curve to make it lie flat. These should not be as deep as the seam allowance. Press the seam gently from the back, then press on the front.

Chain piecing

Chain piecing is a quick way of sewing several sets of patches together. It saves thread, too.

1 Place a pile of pairs of patches with right sides together beside the sewing machine. Sew the first pair along the seam line. At the end of the seam, do not snip the thread but take another couple of stitches beyond the fabric. Feed in the next pair of patches.

2 When you have sewn all the patches, snip the threads to separate the pieced units and press them as usual.

1

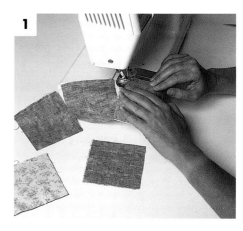

2

◀ West Virginia (page 94) is made from lots of squares and half-square triangles, so the chain piecing technique is ideal for speeding up the sewing process.

Making a block

All of the blocks shown in this book give instructions for the order in which the patches should be sewn together. However, it is not difficult to figure out the most logical order yourself if you start by laying out the patches as they appear in the block you are making, as demonstrated in this example.

1 This block is composed of squares and half-square triangles, so start by joining the patches for all the half-square triangles together.

2 Next, join the squares and pieced squares together in rows. Wherever possible, always arrange the units so that they can be joined in straight rows because this makes sewing easier and you are less likely to make mistakes.

3 Join the rows to complete the block.

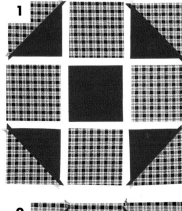

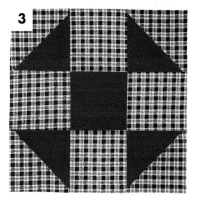

Pressing the block

For greater accuracy, finger-press each seam after you sew it by running a fingernail firmly along the seam line so that it lies in the right direction. The general rule is to press the seam allowance toward the darker fabric so that it does not show through lighter patches. If too many seams join in one place, trim away some of the fabric to make it less bulky or press one seam in a different direction. You may also press the seam open if that works best. When you have finished the block, use an iron to press the block carefully from the back, taking care not to stretch the fabrics. Press down and then lift the iron to reposition it, rather than pushing it over the surface. Turn to the front and press again.

◀ When light and dark patches are joined together, seams are usually pressed toward the darker fabric to keep them from showing through the lighter color.

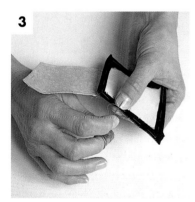

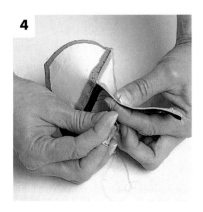

English patchwork

English patchwork, also known as mosaic or paper patchwork, is a method of piecing patches over paper templates. The advantages of this method of patchwork are that it makes it possible to handle fabrics such as silk and satin because the papers anchor them while they are being sewn together. It also makes awkward angles easy, which is one reason for calling it mosaic patchwork— complicated geometric shapes can easily be fitted together just as in mosaic tiles.

1 Make your master templates but do not add a seam allowance. Draw around them on paper and cut out a paper template for each fabric patch. If you need a lot of paper templates, layer three or four papers together at a time.

2 Lay a paper template on a piece of fabric and pin it in place. Cut out the fabric, adding a ¼-inch (6-mm) seam allowance all around. Fold the seam allowance over each edge of the paper and baste all around, folding in the fabric at the corners. Secure each corner with a small backstitch.

3 Place the basted patches right sides together, with edges even. Make a knot in the thread and bring the thread through from the back so that the knot is hidden in the turning. Overcast the edges with small, neat stitches. Finish each seam with a few backstitches and then snip off the thread.

4 To fit a third patch into a tight angle, realign the patches and sew the first seam. Instead of continuing with the same thread, finish off each seam with a few backstitches, snip off the thread, and start the new seam afresh—you will get a stronger join that way. When the patchwork is complete, remove the basting stitches and paper templates, and press gently. If you remove the paper templates carefully, you can reuse them.

◀ The awkward angles of Shaded Trail (page 154) are easier to sew by hand using the English patchwork method.

Foundation piecing

Foundation piecing is a method of piecing blocks by sewing the patches onto foundation fabric. Log Cabin blocks and patterns with lots of strips are often sewn this way because the foundation stabilizes the thin strips and allows more accurate sewing. Use a thin fabric foundation such as fine muslin or cheesecloth, in which case the foundation is left in the blocks, or ordinary paper or special quilting paper that can be torn off when the block is finished.

1 Mark the pattern on one side of the foundation. If there are lots of patches, you may find it helpful to mark the correct stitching order on the foundation. Pin the first patch right side up on the unmarked side of the foundation, making sure that it covers the stitching line completely. The center square of a Basic Log Cabin block is positioned here.

2 Place the first strip on the center patch, right sides together and with edges aligned for the first seam. Check that the strip will cover the next stitching line when pressed open.

3 Turn over the foundation and stitch the seam along the marked line. If you are using a paper foundation, set your machine to 12 stitches per inch (2.5 cm) and always take two or three stitches beyond the marked sewing line to secure each patch. Turn back to the right side and press the strip open.

4 Repeat this process until all the pieces have been added, then remove the foundation if you have used paper, taking care not to pull too roughly on the stitches.

▲ When sewing blocks with many strips of fabric, such as Chevron Log Cabin (page 208), many people find it easier to use the foundation piecing technique.

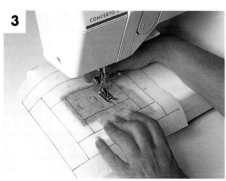

QUICK MARKING TECHNIQUE

If you are making several blocks using a paper foundation, draw the pattern only on the first piece, then place several layers of paper under the top one and pin them together. Remove the thread from the bobbin and from the spool of your sewing machine and stitch over the pattern through all the layers. The needle marks will make a clear and accurate line for you to follow.

Appliqué

Appliqué is a method of making patterns by sewing patches onto a piece of background fabric. It probably began as a means of extending the life of a garment or bedspread, by covering worn areas with patches. It is ideal for creating pictorial designs because curved shapes can be used more easily than in pieced patchwork.

FREEZER PAPER

Use waxed freezer paper to help you achieve crisp edges on your appliqué shapes. Use your templates to cut out patches of freezer paper (do not add a seam allowance).

Place the paper patch onto the wrong side of the fabric, waxed side uppermost. Clip the curves of the fabric patches if necessary, then fold them over the paper patch. Press down the turnings with a dry iron. The fabric will temporarily stick to and be shaped by the paper. Sew the patch in place, leaving a gap to remove the paper. Gently pull the paper through and then close the seam. Alternatively, sew the whole patch down, then cut away the background fabric behind the patch and remove the freezer paper from the back.

Transferring appliqué designs

Make your templates in the usual way, but do not add a seam allowance. Cut out the background fabric, then fold and press it diagonally, vertically, and horizontally. Using the pressed lines as a guide, position the templates on the fabric and draw around them to mark the pattern on the background. Alternatively, if your background fabric is light, you can place it over the appliqué design and trace the design onto the fabric.

Hand appliqué

When you appliqué by hand, you can make the stitching virtually invisible or use a decorative embroidery stitch.

1 Draw around your templates on the required fabric. Cut out the patches, adding a ¼-inch (6-mm) seam allowance all around.

2 Fold under the raw edges, using the drawn lines as a guide. Finger-press the folds firmly, clipping the curves if necessary to make the fabric lie flat. Baste in place. Any edges that will be covered by other patches do not have to be folded under.

3 Pin the patch in place and sew around it. Use a tiny hemming stitch if you want it to be invisible, or try a blanket stitch or a feather stitch for a decorative effect.

Machine appliqué

You can sew appliqué shapes in place by machine in the same way as you do by hand, using a single line of machine straight stitch. Alternatively, you can capitalize on the machine stitching and cover the raw edges of the patches by stitching them with satin stitch or a close zigzag. If you use the latter option, there is no need to add seam allowances to the fabric patches.

1 Patches have a tendency to pucker when stitched by machine, so stabilize the fabric with paper-backed fusible webbing. Place the webbing glue side down on the wrong side of your appliqué fabric. Use your templates to draw around and cut out the required patches.

2 Peel off the paper from the webbing and position the patch on the background fabric. Press with a medium iron to fuse, then sew around the edges in your chosen stitch.

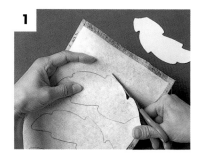

Bias strips

Many appliqué designs feature narrow strips of fabric—for stems in floral designs, for example. Using bias strips for these will achieve a consistent width that lies flat and curves smoothly if necessary. Although not essential, a bias press bar (a flat piece of metal or heat-resistant nylon) will make this job easier. The bar should be the same width as you require the finished bias strips to be.

1 Fold a piece of fabric diagonally in half, making a 45-degree angle, and press.

2 Cut strips of fabric from the resulting triangle. The strips should be twice the required width plus twice the seam allowance.

3 Fold a strip lengthwise, wrong sides together, and sew the seam. To double-check that you are sewing an accurate seam, sew the first 2–3 inches (5–7.5 cm), then insert a bias press bar. Adjust the seam allowance if the strip is narrower or wider than the bar. When you have finished the seam, trim away the excess allowance to about ⅛ inch (3 mm).

4 Roll the tube so that the seam lies down the center, and press flat. To make this easier, push the bias press bar into the tube and twist the fabric around until the seam is on the flat of the bar, then press the bar with a hot iron. Remove the bar and press the bias strip again.

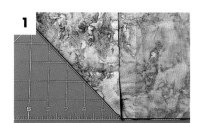

Settings and Layouts

Even the simplest block can produce a remarkable quilt when you explore all the possible ways of laying it out and setting it. Some blocks when simply repeated edge to edge produce interesting secondary patterns—the example shown here is the Compass Quilt block from page 232. The following are some traditional ways of setting blocks into quilts. Refer to pages 36–37 for details different border designs.

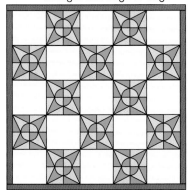

▲ Straight and edge to edge

Set straight and edge to edge

Place two blocks right sides together, matching seams and points, and sew in the usual way using a ¼-inch (6-mm) seam allowance. Press the seam, then continue adding the remaining blocks until your quilt is complete.

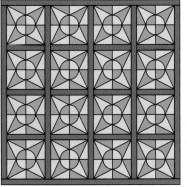

▲ Alternate plain and patterned

Alternate plain and patterned blocks

Alternating pieced or appliquéd blocks with plain ones is a great way of making a few patterned blocks go a long way. The plain areas of fabric also offer the ideal opportunity for interesting quilting patterns that enhance the whole quilt.

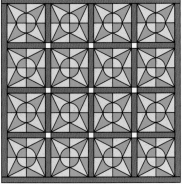

▲ With sashings

Sashings

Sashings are strips of wide or narrow fabric that separate individual blocks. Cut the sashing fabric into strips the same length as the blocks, ensuring that you add seam allowances. Sew the strips and blocks together in columns. Press the columns and measure their length. Cut strips of sashing fabric of this length and join the columns, carefully matching the seam lines of the blocks. If you prefer, you can sew the blocks together in rows, then sew the rows together so that the longer sashing strips go across the quilt rather than down it.

▲ With sashings and posts

Sashings and posts

Posts are squares of fabric positioned at the points where the sashing strips meet. Join columns of blocks with short sashing strips as before. To make the long sashings, cut strips of sashing the same length as the blocks. Cut squares of fabric that are the same width as the sashings. Stitch the sashings and posts together in long strips. Sew the long strips and columns of blocks together, carefully matching the seams so that the corners of the posts meet the corners of the blocks.

Set on point and edge to edge

Blocks can be set on point instead of straight so that they appear as diamonds rather than squares. To do this, stitch the blocks together in rows, but place the rows diagonally across the quilt rather than horizontally. Plan how many blocks you need to sew together for each row, adding half and quarter blocks around the edges to complete the rows as necessary.

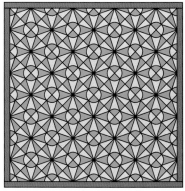

▲ On point and edge to edge

On-point variations

You can use the same setting variations with blocks set on point as you can with straight-set blocks. Separate the rows of blocks with sashings or sashings and posts, or alternate the patterned blocks with plain ones, using plain triangles around the edges instead of half and quarter blocks. You can also set the blocks edge to edge and use plain triangles just around the edges; this arrangement can be set with or without sashings and posts. You can even combine on-point blocks with straight sashings and posts. To do this, set the patterned blocks on point and add a plain triangle to each side to make them into large squares, then join these with sashings and posts.

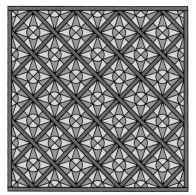

▲ With sashings

▲ With sashings and posts

▲ Alternate plain and patterned with sashings

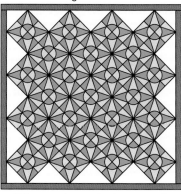

▲ Edge to edge with plain triangles around the edges

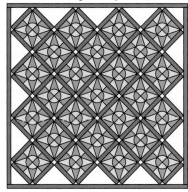

▲ With sashings, posts, and plain triangles around the edges

OTHER VARIATIONS

Remember also that you can rotate the blocks within the quilt top—you will find lots of variations in the next chapter demonstrating this. You can also combine more than one block in the same quilt.

Borders

Not every quilt needs a border, but borders can often set off the blocks and considerably enhance the quilt top. There are several types of borders: strips can be added to the top, bottom, and sides and finished with straight seams, corner posts, or mitered (diagonal) seams. Other options are to make pieced borders or use several borders together.

▲ Plain border

▲ Multiple borders

▲ With corner posts

▲ With multiple posts

Plain border

Measure the width and length of the quilt. It is best to do this across the center of the quilt because the edges may have become stretched with handling. Cut two strips the same length as the quilt plus seam allowances. Sew these to the sides of the quilt and press. Cut two more strips the same width as the quilt plus the width of the first two border strips and seam allowances. Sew these to the top and bottom of the quilt and press. If you prefer, you could add the top and bottom border strips first, then add the side pieces.

Multiple borders

Many quilts look best when they are framed by multiple borders. You could alternate plain and patterned borders, or narrow and wide ones. This is a good way of making sure that there is sufficient contrast between the colors in the main field of the quilt and the fabric you want to use for the main border. By adding a narrow strip in a strongly contrasting fabric, you will visually separate the main border from the quilt.

Border with posts

Cut two strips the same width as the quilt and two strips the same length, adding seam allowances. Cut four squares the same width as the border strips, with seam allowances. Sew a strip to each side of the quilt. Add a corner post to each end of the other two strips and press. Sew the top and bottom border strips to the quilt and press. You can add a post at each junction of the blocks along the whole length of the border strips. To do this, make the border pieces in the same way as you would make long pieces of sashings and posts (see page 34), then sew them to the quilt as usual.

Mitered border

Mitered borders frame a quilt like a picture frame and are particularly attractive when using striped fabrics. The secret is not to stitch into the seam allowances at the corners. Measure the length and width of the quilt top and cut strips, adding a generous allowance of at least twice the width of the border.

1 Pin and stitch the border strips to the edge of the quilt on all four sides, leaving an equal amount of extra fabric at each end. Stop the stitching at the seam allowance in each corner, securing the ends of each line of sewing with a small backstitch. Press the border open and lay out the quilt on a flat surface. Let the extensions overlap each other and turn under the top one at an angle of 45 degrees. Press the fold well.

2 Fold the quilt with the right sides of the border together and stitch along the pressed line from the inner to the outer corner. Trim away the excess and press the seam open.

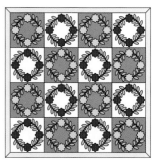

▲ Mitered border

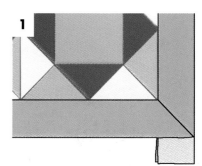

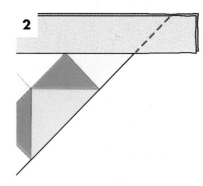

Pieced border

You can make border strips from pieced patches instead of lengths of fabric. Try to relate the pieces in the border to elements in the blocks, both by size and shape, so that the border complements the block design. You may even be able to use leftover patches from the blocks to make a border. Many pieced border designs are named just like blocks, or you could create your own unique design.

▲ Narrow mitered border framed by a border of pieced diamonds.

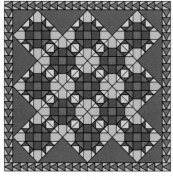

▲ Flying Geese border pieced from three-triangle units.

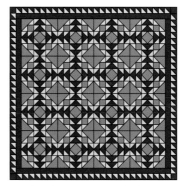

▲ Plain border surrounded by a Sawtooth border pieced from leftover patches from the blocks.

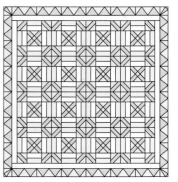

▲ Plain inner border with outer Dogstooth border.

Quilting Designs

Once you have completed the quilt top, the next stage is to assemble it into a quilt with a layer of batting and backing fabric. These need to be secured together by sewing through all three layers with a quilting design. There are numerous styles to choose from. A few ideas are given here.

EMBELLISHING QUILTS

You can embellish quilts in all sorts of ways in addition to the traditional quilting techniques described here. This quilt is embellished with a variety of decorative embroidery stitches and beads, but you can also use sequins, lace, and ribbons.

Stitch-in-the-ditch quilting

The quilting stitches are made directly over the seam lines, so they are almost invisible in the finished quilt but help to define the pieced or appliquéd shapes and anchor the layers together.

Outline quilting

Lines of quilting stitches are made around the pieced shapes, usually ¼ inch (6 mm) away from the patches. You can draw guidelines on the quilt with removable fabric marker.

Echo quilting

Several rows of quilting stitches follow the outline of patches, echoing their shapes across the quilt surface. This is especially effective with appliqué blocks.

Stipple quilting

Also called random, meander, or vermicelli quilting, stipple quilting involves filling areas with a random design. It is usually sewn "freehand" with a sewing machine, without marking the design on the fabric first.

Medallion designs

There are numerous medallion designs that you can use to embellish your quilt. They are ideal for large patches, alternating plain blocks, and posts.

Tulips

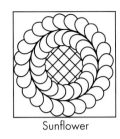
Sunflower

Spiral daisy

Celtic knot

Border patterns

Like medallions, traditional border designs are often based on shapes such as flowers, stars, and feathers. Braids, waves, and twisted cables are also popular.

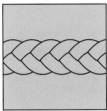
Braid

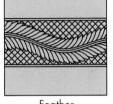
Feather

Heart swag

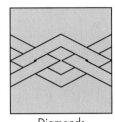
Diamonds

Background designs

Background designs provide a general texture that creates a visual contrast to the main motifs of the quilt.

Rainbows

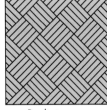

Basketweave

Spirals

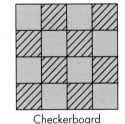
Checkerboard

▸ This quilt has been handsewn with floral medallion designs in the center square and corner posts. The outer border features large symmetrical feather motifs, while a single line of stitches in a wave design is used in both inner borders. The turquoise fabric surrounding the center square is quilted with a background grid of diagonal stitching.

Quilting Techniques

Once you have chosen your quilting design, the next stage is to mark the design on the quilt top and assemble the quilt. This involves creating a "quilt sandwich" with the quilt top, batting, and backing fabric. You can then sew the quilting design by hand or machine.

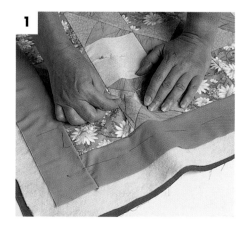

Transferring quilting designs

There are numerous ways of marking a design onto the quilt top, including tracing and using templates.

1 To trace a design, draw the pattern in black pen, then fix it to a table or other flat surface with masking tape. Place the quilt top over the pattern and anchor it with masking tape. Trace the pattern onto the quilt top, using either a soft pencil or any other marker that can be removed easily after quilting. White quilt-marking pencils are good for marking dark fabrics.

2 There are also many ready-made quilting templates available that you can trace around, or you can make your own.

Making the quilt sandwich

Measure the quilt top and cut the batting and backing fabric at least 2 inches (5 cm) larger all around.

1 Smooth the three layers together on a flat surface and pin together with large, glass-headed pins. Baste together with big stitches, starting at the center and working outward. Work across the quilt and then top to bottom, or work out diagonally.

2 A quicker way of securing the quilt sandwich is to use safety pins to anchor the layers together. Again, start at the center and work outward, placing the pins at regular intervals.

TRACING TIPS
If the quilting pattern does not show through when you try to trace it—under dark fabrics, for example—fix the pattern to a window with masking tape and fix the quilt over it. You can also improvise a light box by supporting a sheet of glass on piles of books and placing a lamp beneath it.

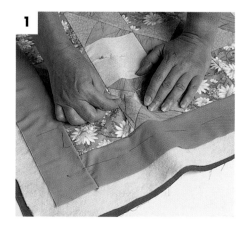

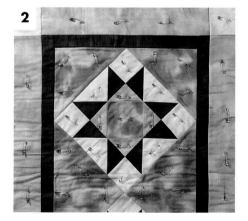

Hand quilting

The hand-quilting stitch is a simple running stitch, but the stitches must go through all three layers of the quilt and must be as even as possible. Evenness is more important than the size of the stitch. Wear a thimble on the second finger of the hand you stitch with; a thimble with a small ridge around the crown is best. Use a quilting needle (between) and quilting thread. Running the thread through beeswax will strengthen it and prevent knotting.

1 Place a quilting hoop over one section of the quilt and fasten it so that the quilt fabric is taut. To quilt right up to the edges of the quilt, baste some strips of plain fabric to the edges so that the hoop can extend right over the area to be quilted. When one section of quilting is complete, move the hoop to the next section.

2 Make a knot in the quilting thread and push the needle up from the back of the quilt, until the knot pops through into the batting. Take a small backstitch. Begin quilting by pushing the needle through all three layers, keeping it as straight as possible. Keep your nonstitching hand under the place where you are working and use your finger to push up the fabric just in front of the needle. You should feel the point of the needle at each stitch. Use a finger guard if your finger becomes sore. Take several stitches before pulling the thread through. Aim at a light rocking motion with the needle, best achieved by lodging the needle against the thimble. At the end of the thread, make a knot and take a small backstitch. Push the needle into the batting and bring it out a short distance away. Pull the thread gently until the knot pops into the backing. Snip off the thread closely.

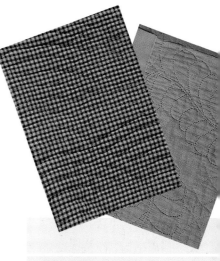

BACKING FABRIC
The quilting design will be visible on the back of your finished quilt, and adds an extra decorative feature to the quilt. However, if you do not want it to be visible, you could choose a backing fabric that will camouflage the quilting, such as a checked or floral fabric. Alternatively, you could use a piece of cheesecloth or similar fabric as backing while you are quilting, then attach a separate backing when the quilting is finished

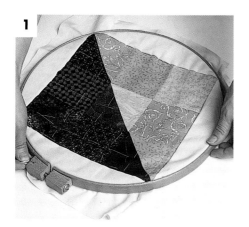

Straight machine quilting

Use this technique for patterns that can be stitched in straight lines or gentle curves. Mark the fabric with the quilting design if necessary and prepare the quilt layers exactly as for hand quilting. Attach an even-feed foot or walking foot to your machine and use machine needle no. 12 (US) or no. 80 (European). It is a good idea to make a practice piece first.

1 Place your hands on either side of the piece you are about to quilt and press down gently but firmly. Quilt straight lines, starting and ending each row with a couple of backstitches. Check that the fabric does not pucker, and adjust the tension on the machine if necessary. Quilt across the first lines to make squares and check the fabric for puckering once again. Keep adjusting the tension and stitch length until you are happy with the result.

2 Try stitching some gentle curves, using your hands to ease the quilt into position. When stitching is complete, thread the ends through a needle, draw them through the fabric layers, and bring them up at the back of the quilt to tie off and snip.

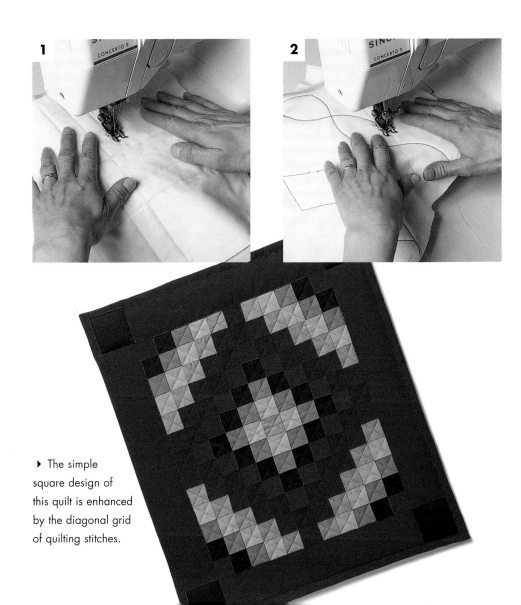

GETTING A GRIP
Soft cotton gardening gloves with small rubber dots on the underside make it easy to grip the quilt as you work.

▶ The simple square design of this quilt is enhanced by the diagonal grid of quilting stitches.

Free machine quilting

Use this technique for patterns with more exaggerated curves. Either drop the feed dogs or cover them with a special plate, depending on your machine. Fit a darning foot or special quilting foot if you have one, set the stitch length at 0, and loosen the tension slightly. It is important that you learn how to control the speed and movement of the work, so make some practice pieces.

1 Begin by taking a single stitch, turning the wheel manually, then bring the thread from the bobbin up to the top. This will ensure it does not snarl up as you begin stitching. Begin sewing, running the machine at a slightly slower rate than usual. The feed dogs are disconnected, so you will have to move the quilt under the needle. Move it as evenly and steadily as possible—too fast and the stitches will be too small, too slow and the stitches will be too large.

2 Practice sewing some random patterns (known as stipple or meander quilting). This is a very useful technique, so it is worth spending some time to master it.

TRACING PAPER
Instead of marking the quilting design directly onto the quilt, you could draw it on tracing paper, pin the paper to the quilt top, and stitch through the paper. Tear the paper away when the quilting is finished.

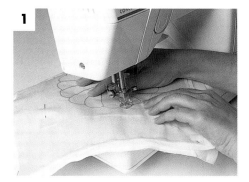

Tying a quilt

To tie the layers of the quilt together instead of applying a quilting design, use a long needle and strong thread such as perle cotton or embroidery silk. Push the needle through all three layers from front to back, leaving a tail of about 2 inches (5 cm) on the quilt top. Bring the needle back to the top very close to where it went in. Take another stitch like this and snip off, again leaving a tail of thread. Tie the ends together in a knot, then trim to about 1 inch (2.5 cm) or less. Repeat at regular intervals across the quilt.

▶ You can use decorative buttons to tie a quilt instead of thread if you wish.

The Quilt Recipes

The hardest thing in this chapter is deciding which quilt to make, so use the handy contents listing on the following pages to help you choose. All 100 quilt blocks are pictured together so you can compare and contrast them. The blocks are organized into 10 categories, from simple all-over designs and geometric blocks to log cabins and appliqué patterns— there's something to suit everyone's taste.

100 Blocks At a Glance

This chapter features 100 fabulous quilt blocks. All 100 are displayed here to help you choose the ones you want to make. Use the page references to take you to the step-by-step recipes for each block.

ONE- AND TWO-PATCH BLOCKS

Woven Patchwork *p. 52*

Chevrons *p. 54*

Grandmother's Flower Garden *p. 56*

London Stairs *p. 58*

One-patch Star *p. 60*

FOUR-PATCH BLOCKS

Economy *p. 62*

Road to Oklahoma *p. 64*

Pinwheel Square *p. 66*

Left and Right *p. 68*

Cross in a Cross *p. 70*

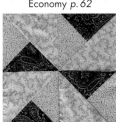
Broken Pinwheel *p. 72*

Missouri Star *p. 74*

Snail Trail *p. 76*

Dogstooth Violet *p. 78*

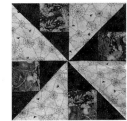
Brave World *p. 80*

Windblown Square *p. 82*

Old Maid's Ramble *p. 84*

Crossed Canoes *p. 86*

Squares and Stripes *p. 88*

Flock of Geese *p. 90*

1904 Star *p. 92*

West Virginia *p. 94*

Bridal Path *p. 96*

FIVE-PATCH BLOCKS

Butterfly at the Crossroads *p.98*

Handy Andy *p.100*

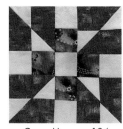
Bachelor's Puzzle *p.102*

Crazy House *p.104*

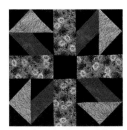
Jack in the Box *p.106*

Single Wedding Ring *p.108*

Domino *p.110*

Grape Basket *p.112*

Grandmother's Cross *p.114*

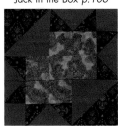
Queen Charlotte's Crown *p.116*

Leap Frog *p.118*

Goose Tracks *p.120*

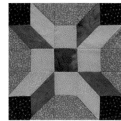
Wild Rose and Square *p.122*

Crazy Ann *p.124*

Biloxi Variation *p.126*

SEVEN-PATCH BLOCKS

Bear's Paw *p.128*

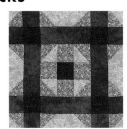
Greek Cross *p.130*

Seven-patch Mosaic *p.132*

Buffalo Ridge Quilt *p.134*

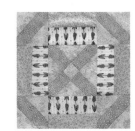
Girl's Joy *p.136*

Dove at the Window *p.138*

Stonemason's Puzzle *p.140*

Seven-patch Flower *p.142*

NINE-PATCH BLOCKS

Stepping Stones *p.144*

Locked Star *p.146*

Memory *p.148*

"A" Star Variation *p.150*

Roman Pavement *p.152*

Shaded Trail *p.154*

Four Corners *p.156*

Ocean Waves *p.158*

Rolling Stone *p.160*

Basket of Scraps *p.162*

Doris's Delight *p.164*

Box Quilt *p.166*

Puss in the Corner *p.168*

Weather Vane *p.170*

Maltese Star *p.172*

Claws Variation *p.174*

Joseph's Coat *p.176*

Arrows *p.178*

Wyoming Valley *p.180*

Star Diamond *p.182*

Illinois *p.184*

Dolley Madison's Star *p.186*

Braced Star *p.188*

Calico Puzzle *p.190*

Garden Maze *p.192*

EIGHT-POINTED STARS

Compass Kaleidoscope *p.194*

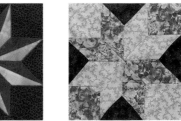

Star of the East *p.196*

Sunshine and Shadow *p.198*

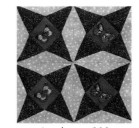

Amethyst *p.200*

Star Upon Stars *p.202*

Arkensas Traveler *p.204*

LOG CABIN BLOCKS

Basic Log Cabin *p. 206*

Chevron Log Cabin *p. 208*

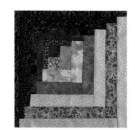

Courthouse Steps *p. 210*

Off-center Log Cabin *p. 212*

BLOCKS WITH CURVES

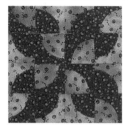

Drunkard's Path *p. 214*

Orange Peel *p. 216*

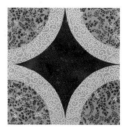

Circular Saw *p. 218*

Broken Stone *p. 220*

Suspension Bridge *p. 222*

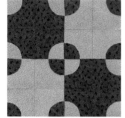

Mill Wheel *p. 224*

Pincushion *p. 226*

Double Wedding Ring *p. 228*

Hands All Around *p. 230*

Compass Quilt *p. 232*

Bleeding Hearts *p. 234*

FAN BLOCKS

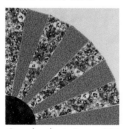

Grandmother's Fan *p. 236*

Japanese Fan *p. 238*

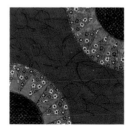

Snake Trail *p. 240*

APPLIQUE BLOCKS

Peonies *p. 242*

Rose of Sharon *p. 244*

Oak Leaf Wreath *p. 246*

Triple Flower *p. 248*

Mexican Rose *p. 250.*

SKILL LEVEL ▾

TEMPLATE ▾

A

Woven Patchwork

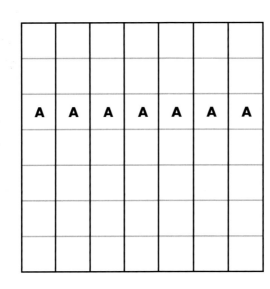

This simple block can produce lots of different patterns. Here, alternate blocks are rotated 90 degrees, producing a Basketweave pattern, and the quilt is finished with bound edges. Although this example has seven strips, you can use more or fewer if you wish—just draft the block on a different grid. The fabrics are placed symmetrically around a dark central strip in this quilt, but you can mix and match them as you please.

FABRICS ▾

| 4 | 3 | 2 | 1 | 2 | 3 | 4 |

1 DARK
2 MEDIUM LIGHT
3 MEDIUM DARK
4 LIGHT

A A A A A A A

Drafting

Draft the block on a 7 × 7 grid and make the template.

Make a quick sketch of the block and pin scraps of your fabrics to it to use as reference.

Making the block

1 When handling long strips of fabric that might be difficult to stitch accurately, press the fabric well and use spray starch to stabilize it. Cut out all the fabric in the required shape as directed.

A

Cut 1 of Fabric 1
Cut 2 of Fabric 2
Cut 2 of Fabric 3
Cut 2 of Fabric 4

2 Join the first pair of strips.

3 Continue adding strips to complete the block.

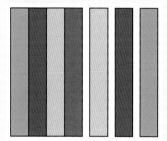

4 If you are making lots of blocks using the same fabrics, save time by cutting long strips of each fabric in the required width. Join the strips to form a long band, then cut the band into sections of the required length.

Variations

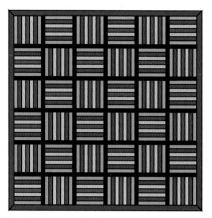

Blocks set in a Basketweave pattern with narrow dark sashings and a mitered border.

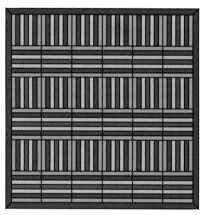

Alternate rows of blocks are rotated 90 degrees instead of alternate blocks.

Blocks set on point, with alternate rows rotated 90 degrees. The quilt is finished with plain triangles around the edges and a mitered border.

SKILL LEVEL ▾

TEMPLATES ▾

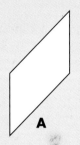

A

B

FABRICS ▾

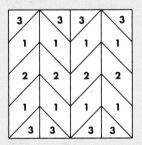

1 *DARK*
2 *MEDIUM*
3 *LIGHT*

Chevrons

The chevron is a very old pattern, probably derived from the shape made by the meeting of eaves on a roof. As well as featuring frequently on coats of arms and old floor tiles, quilters have exploited the chevron's design value to produce some interesting effects. Other names for this block include Building Blocks, Wave, and Rail Fence. This example is finished with a border and corner posts.

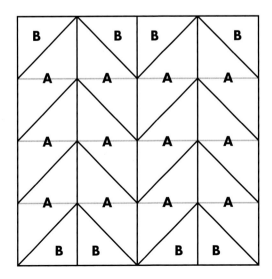

Drafting

Draft the block on a 4 × 4 grid and make the templates.

Make a quick sketch of the block and pin scraps of your fabrics to it to use as reference.

Making the block

1 Cut out all the fabric in the required shapes as directed.

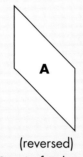

B

Cut 8 of Fabric 3

A

Cut 4 of Fabric 1
Cut 2 of Fabric 2

A

(reversed)
Cut 4 of Fabric 1
Cut 2 of Fabric 2

2 Join the patches in columns to make two of each design.

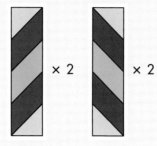

× 2   × 2

3 Join pairs of columns together.

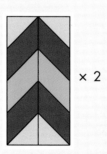

× 2

4 Join the two pieced units to complete the block.

Variations

By rotating alternate rows of blocks 180 degrees, a pattern of squares appears between them.

The same design set with sashings and posts. Now the squares appear to be lying under a grid.

This variation is known as Herringbone. By building up columns of chevrons and finishing them with triangles at top and bottom, the resulting pattern looks like piled-up boxes. Using a variety of dark and light fabrics makes this an excellent scrap quilt.

SKILL LEVEL ▾

TEMPLATE ▾

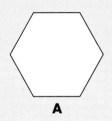

A

FABRICS ▾

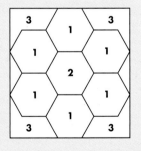

1 MEDIUM LIGHT
2 LIGHT
3 DARK

Grandmother's Flower Garden

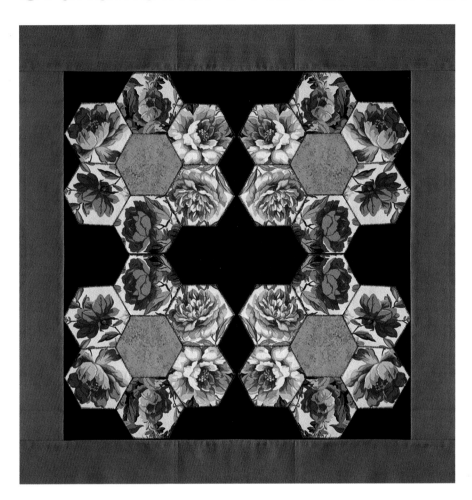

Generations of children have learned to make patchwork using this pattern, but do not underestimate its design potential—in this version, the flowers are appliquéd to a background square, with the edges of the flowers meeting to produce interesting subsidiary patterns in the background fabric. The quilt is finished with a plain border. Use the English patchwork method to piece it (see page 30).

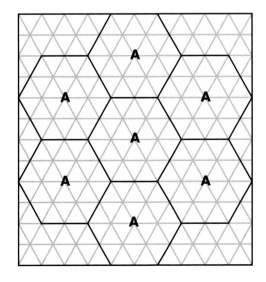

Drafting

Draft the block on an isometric grid and make the template.

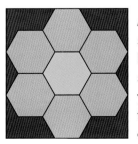

Make a quick sketch of the block and pin scraps of your fabrics to it to use as reference.

Making the block

✂

1 Cut out Fabric 1 in the required shape as directed. When cutting the paper patches, do not add a seam allowance. Cut a background square of Fabric 3 at the size of the finished block, plus a seam allowance.

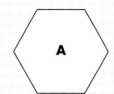

Cut 6 of Fabric 1
Cut 1 of Fabric 2
Cut 7 of paper

2 Make all the A patches either by basting the fabric in place if you are using ordinary paper (see page 30) or by pressing it into position if you are using freezer paper (see page 32).

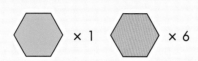

3 Stitch six petals around the center patch.

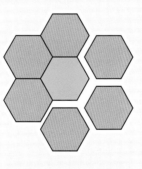

4 Pin the flower centrally onto the background square and appliqué it in place by stitching around each petal to complete the block.

Variations

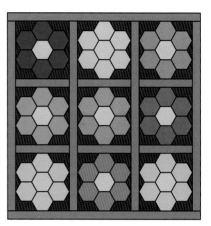

Flower blocks in a variety of fabrics set with sashings. This classic scrap quilt is unified by the black background squares, the use of the same color for the center of each flower, and the monotone border and sashings.

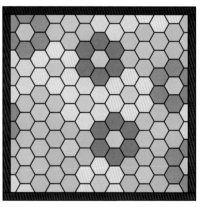

For a traditional "all-over" quilt, omit the background squares and join the flowers edge to edge. Build up the pattern until it is the size you need, then add a border, cutting off any excess patches or half patches around the edges. Regular and random arrangements of colors both work well.

SKILL LEVEL ▾

TEMPLATE ▾

A

FABRICS ▾

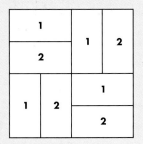

1 DARK
2 LIGHT

London Stairs

Some of the simplest patchwork patterns can make stunning quilts. The piecing of this block is as easy as it gets, but the result can look deceptively complex. It can be designed in just two fabrics—a light and a dark—or make it as a wonderful scrap quilt by simply sorting your fabrics into light and dark shades. This example is finished with a border and corner posts.

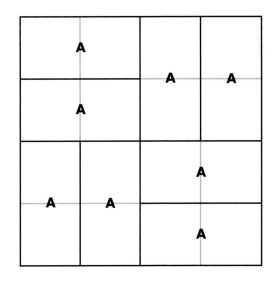

Drafting

Draft the block on a 4 × 4 grid and make the template.

Make a quick sketch of the block and pin scraps of your fabrics to it to use as reference.

Making the block

✂

1 Cut out all the fabric in the required shape as directed.

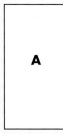

Cut 4 of Fabric 1
Cut 4 of Fabric 2

2 Join pairs of patches together.

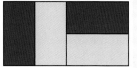 × 4

3 Join pairs of pieced units, rotating them to form the pattern.

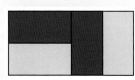

4 Join the rows to complete the block.

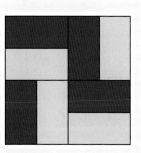

Variations

Each block has been rotated 90 degrees clockwise, so that the stairs appear to rise instead of descend from left to right. The sashings and border frame the individual blocks.

Groups of four London Stairs blocks can be rotated and flipped to create a new block, known as the Keyhole block. This quilt is composed of 16 Keyhole blocks and is an excellent scrap quilt, with a strong graphic effect.

One-patch Star

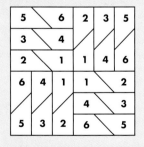

This ingenious use of a tesselated shape is essentially a way of using lots of scraps of fabric because each block can be worked in a different color group. Even if you repeat the same fabrics in each block, you will create an interesting pattern. The block is constructed from four identical units, each one rotated 90 degrees to form the star in the center, and the quilt is finished with a plain border.

Drafting

Draft the block on a 6 × 6 grid and make the template.

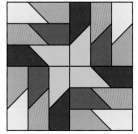

Make a quick sketch of the block and pin scraps of your fabrics to it to use as reference.

Making the block

1 Cut out all the fabric in the required shape as directed.

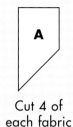

Cut 4 of
each fabric

2 Join pairs of patches in the color combinations shown.

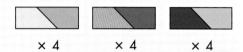

× 4 × 4 × 4

3 Join the pieced patches to form the corner units.

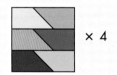

× 4

4 Join pairs of units together, rotating them to form a star in the center.

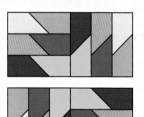

5 Join the rows to complete the block.

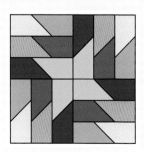

Variations

When the blocks are set with sashings, the light-colored patches form stars that seem to spill out from under the grid.

Blocks set with sashings and posts in a contrasting color.

Blocks set on point with plain triangles around the edges and a plain border.

Economy

SKILL LEVEL ▾

TEMPLATES ▾

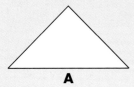

A

B

Perhaps the name of this block, first published toward the end of the nineteenth century, evokes the spirit of the early American quilt makers, who would have used every scrap of fabric to create warm and durable bedcovers. The visual impression is of two different pieced blocks: a square within a square and a pinwheel block. The quilt is finished with a border and corner posts.

FABRICS ▾

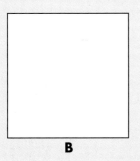

1 *MEDIUM*
2 *LIGHT*
3 *DARK*
4 *FEATURE*

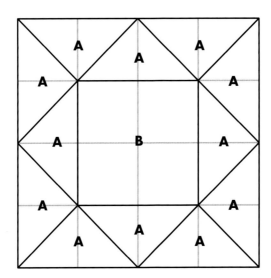

Drafting

Draft the block on a 4 × 4 grid and make the templates.

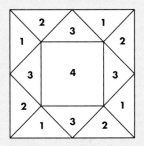

Make a quick sketch of the block and pin scraps of your fabrics to it to use as reference.

Making the block

1 Cut out all the fabric in the required shapes as directed.

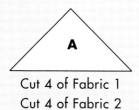

Cut 4 of Fabric 1
Cut 4 of Fabric 2
Cut 4 of Fabric 3

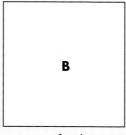

Cut 1 of Fabric 4

2 Join a Fabric 3 patch to each side of the Fabric 4 patch to make the center square.

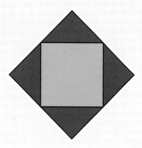

3 Join pairs of Fabric 1 and 2 patches together to make the corner units.

 × 4

4 Lay out the corner units around the center square.

5 Join the units to complete the block.

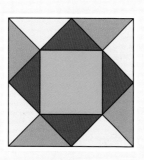

Variations

Sashings and posts disrupt the visual impact of the pinwheel blocks, although they can still be seen underneath the grid if you look carefully.

Blocks set on point with plain triangles around the edges.

Blocks set on point with alternate plain squares. The quilt is finished with plain triangles around the edges.

Road to Oklahoma

SKILL LEVEL ▾

TEMPLATES ▾

A

B

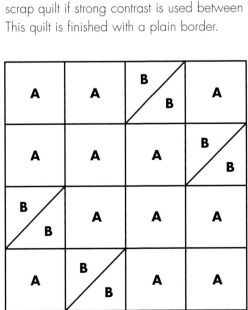

Road to Oklahoma is a good example of the way in which an easy block can be used to make a stunning quilt. The strong diagonal emphasis means that interesting subsidiary patterns emerge when blocks are repeated. This block makes an effective scrap quilt if strong contrast is used between the light, medium, and dark fabrics. This quilt is finished with a plain border.

FABRICS ▾

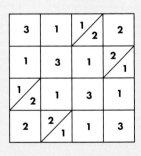

1 LIGHT
2 DARK
3 MEDIUM

Drafting

Draft the block on a 4 × 4 grid and make the templates.

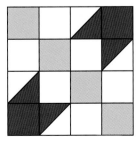

Make a quick sketch of the block and pin scraps of your fabrics to it to use as reference.

Making the block

✄

1 Cut out all the fabric in the required shapes as directed.

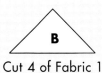

Cut 6 of Fabric 1
Cut 2 of Fabric 2
Cut 4 of Fabric 3

Cut 4 of Fabric 1
Cut 4 of Fabric 2

2 Join pairs of B patches together.

 × 4

3 Join the A patches and pieced units in rows.

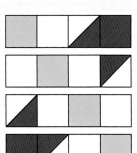

4 Join the rows to complete the block.

Variations

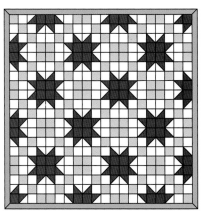

When alternate blocks are rotated 90 degrees, a pattern of stars emerges.

Rotated blocks set with sashings and posts, so that the stars appear to emerge from beneath a grid.

SKILL LEVEL ▾

TEMPLATES ▾

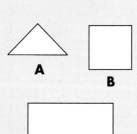

A

B

C

D

E

FABRICS ▾

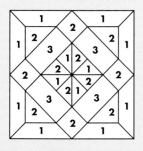

1 MEDIUM
2 DARK
3 LIGHT

Pinwheel Square

Pinwheel blocks are an old favorite with quilt makers, and there are many different variations. This pattern offers some interesting design effects that are enhanced by the mitered corners of the individual blocks. Mitered corners require careful piecing, but otherwise the block is relatively straightforward to make. This example is finished with a plain border.

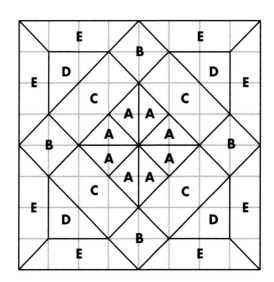

Drafting

Draft the block on an 8 × 8 grid and make the templates.

Make a quick sketch of the block and pin scraps of your fabrics to it to use as reference.

Making the block

✂

1 Cut out all the fabric in the required shapes as directed.

A
Cut 4 of Fabric 1
Cut 4 of Fabric 2

B
Cut 4 of Fabric 2

C
Cut 4 of Fabric 3

D
Cut 4 of Fabric 2

E
Cut 8 of Fabric 1

2 Join pairs of Fabric 1 A and 2 A patches together, then join the four units, rotating each unit 90 degrees.

3 Lay out the pieced unit with the B and C patches and join them in rows, then join the rows to complete the center square.

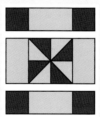

4 Join two E patches to each D patch, setting in the seams at the mitered corner (see page 27).

× 4

5 With the center square set on point, lay out the corner units around it. Join them to complete the block.

Variations

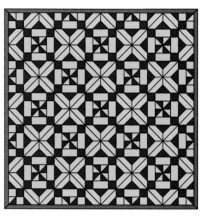

When blocks are set on point, the emphasis is on the central squares. The E patches at the edges of the blocks form diagonal crosses.

The dark border and sashings make an effective frame for the individual blocks.

Left and Right

SKILL LEVEL ▾

TEMPLATES ▾

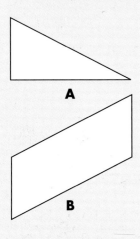

A

B

This intriguing block from the 1930s has a distinctly modern look. It is the sort of pattern seen in Victorian floor tiles, and the colors used here are typical of those that would have been used for that purpose. When repeated blocks are set together, an interesting three-dimensional pattern of boxed tiles appears. The trick is to use dark and light tones of the same color for the bands. The quilt is finished with a plain border.

FABRICS ▾

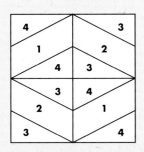

1 *MEDIUM LIGHT*
2 *MEDIUM DARK*
3 *LIGHT*
4 *DARK*

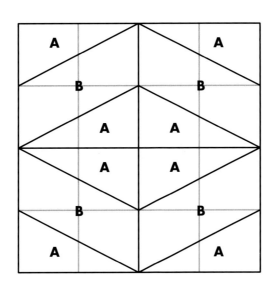

Drafting

Draft the block on a 4 × 4 grid and make the templates.

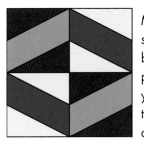

Make a quick sketch of the block and pin scraps of your fabrics to it to use as reference.

Making the block

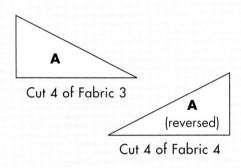

1 Cut out all the fabric in the required shapes as directed.

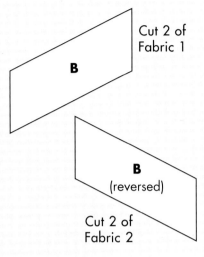

Cut 4 of Fabric 3

Cut 4 of Fabric 4

B
Cut 2 of Fabric 1

B (reversed)
Cut 2 of Fabric 2

2 Join two Fabric 4 patches to each Fabric 1 patch.

 × 2

3 Join two Fabric 3 patches to each Fabric 2 patch.

 × 2

4 Join the units in pairs.

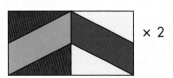 × 2

5 Join the pairs to complete the block, rotating the lower pair to form the pattern.

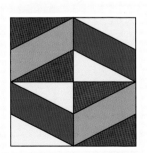

Variations

Blocks set with monotone sashings, posts, and a mitered border.

Blocks set on point with plain triangles around the edges and a plain border.

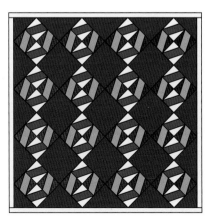

Blocks set on point with alternate plain squares and triangles.

SKILL LEVEL ▾

TEMPLATES ▾

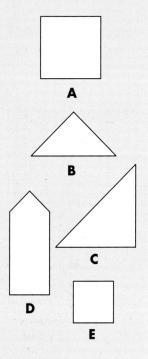

A

B

C

D

E

FABRICS ▾

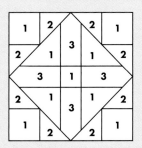

1 *LIGHT*
2 *DARK*
3 *MEDIUM*

Cross in a Cross

Many blocks dating from the nineteenth century have names that reflect the religious times in which they originated, so there are several blocks featuring crosses. Cross in a Cross is easy to piece if you construct the center square as a separate unit. This quilt, finished with a mitered border, features repeated blocks set side by side in rows, which produces an interesting subsidiary pattern.

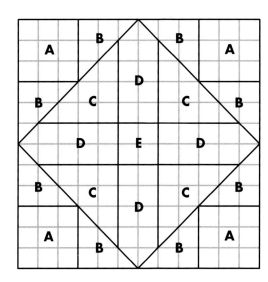

Drafting

Draft the block on a 12 × 12 grid and make the templates.

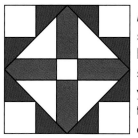

Make a quick sketch of the block and pin scraps of your fabrics to it to use as reference.

Making the block

✄

1 Cut out all the fabric in the required shapes as directed.

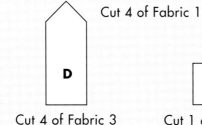

A
Cut 4 of Fabric 1

B
Cut 8 of Fabric 2

C
Cut 4 of Fabric 1

D
Cut 4 of Fabric 3

E
Cut 1 of Fabric 1

2 Join two B patches to each A patch to make the corner units.

× 4

3 Join the C, D, and E patches.

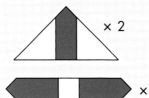
× 2

× 1

4 Join the center square elements together.

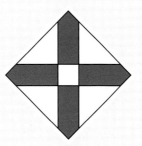

5 Join a corner unit to each side of the center square to complete the block.

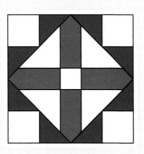

Variations

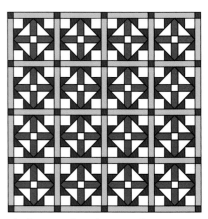

Blocks set with sashings and contrasting colored posts.

Blocks set on point with sashings, posts, and a plain border. Half and quarter blocks are used around the outer edges.

Broken Pinwheel

SKILL LEVEL ▾

TEMPLATES ▾

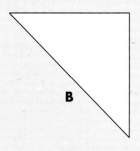

A

B

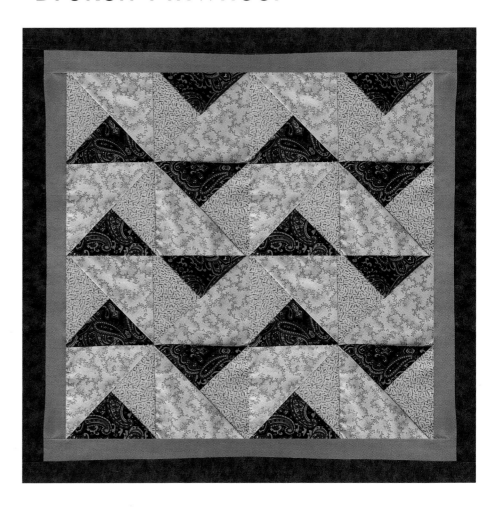

Pinwheel blocks always look effective, even as scrap quilts. A light fabric has been used for the large triangles in this block, but you could choose a dark fabric instead, with a medium and light fabric for the two smaller triangles. The two smaller triangles could also be made using two medium-shaded fabrics, as long as there is a good contrast between them. A double border provides a decorative frame to the quilt.

FABRICS ▾

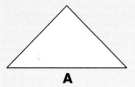

1 *MEDIUM*
2 *DARK*
3 *LIGHT*

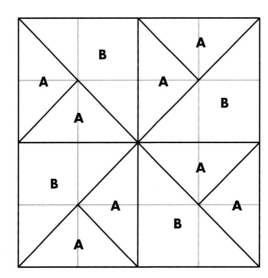

Drafting

Draft the block on a 4 × 4 grid and make the templates.

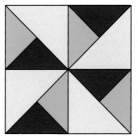

Make a quick sketch of the block and pin scraps of your fabrics to it to use as reference.

Making the block

1 Cut out all the fabric in the required shapes as directed.

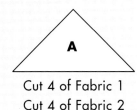

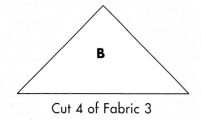

Cut 4 of Fabric 1
Cut 4 of Fabric 2

Cut 4 of Fabric 3

2 Join pairs of A patches together.

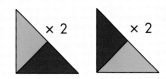

× 2 × 2

3 Join a B patch to each pieced unit.

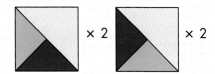

× 2 × 2

4 Join the pieced units in pairs, rotating them to form the pattern.

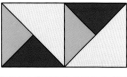

5 Join the pairs to complete the block.

Variations

Blocks set with sashings, posts, and a single border.

A new pattern is made by organizing the small triangles so that patches of a single color meet in the center of the block. As a result, the large triangles appear to overlap a square. This effect is emphasized if a dark color is used for the large triangles.

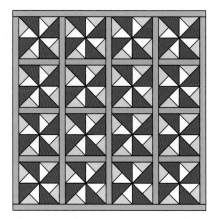

The same color organization is used here, but this time the blocks are separated by sashings.

Snail Trail

SKILL LEVEL ▾

TEMPLATES ▾

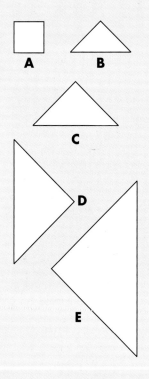

A B

C

D

E

FABRICS ▾

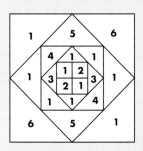

1 LIGHT
2–6 MEDIUM
TO DARK

Snail Trail is also known as Indiana Puzzle, Virginia Wheel, and Whirligig. You can get several different patterns by experimenting with the colors. Here, just one fabric has been used for all the light patches, but you can vary the light fabrics as well as the dark tones if you like. The only important thing is for there to be a good contrast between the light and dark fabrics. This quilt is finished with a border and corner posts.

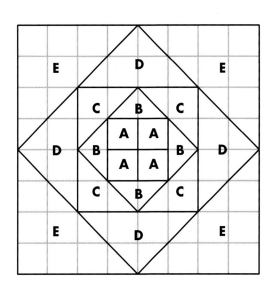

Drafting

Draft the block on an 8 × 8 grid and make the templates.

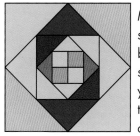

Make a quick sketch of the block and pin scraps of your fabrics to it to use as reference.

Making the block

1 Cut out all the fabric in the required shapes as directed.

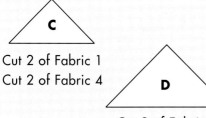
A Cut 2 of Fabric 1
Cut 2 of Fabric 2

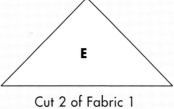
B Cut 2 of Fabric 1
Cut 2 of Fabric 3

C Cut 2 of Fabric 1
Cut 2 of Fabric 4

D Cut 2 of Fabric 1
Cut 2 of Fabric 5

E Cut 2 of Fabric 1
Cut 2 of Fabric 6

2 Join the A patches together to make the center square.

3 Join a B patch to each side of the square, with patches of the same fabric opposite each other.

4 Repeat this process with the C patches.

5 Join the D patches in the same way, then finally add the E patches to complete the block.

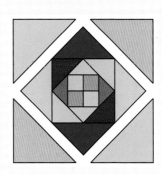

Variations

When alternate blocks are rotated 90 degrees, a completely different pattern emerges.

Rotated blocks set with sashings, border, and posts.

Dogstooth Violet

TEMPLATES ▾

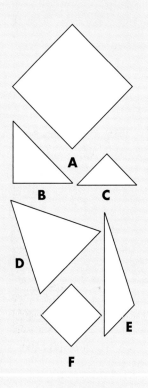

FABRICS ▾

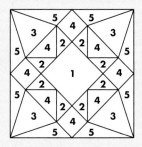

1 *FEATURE*
2 *DARK*
3 *MEDIUM DARK*
4 *MEDIUM LIGHT*
5 *LIGHT*

Dogstooth Violet is the common name given to the garden flower *Erythronium*, the shape of whose petals echoes the triangles in the four corners of this block. It is a beautiful block that, when repeated, produces the effect of interlocking circles. This example is finished with a mitered border. The center square provides the opportunity to use a striking feature fabric, the floral motif used here being particularly apt.

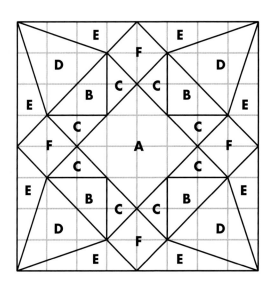

Drafting

Draft the block on an 8 × 8 grid and make the templates.

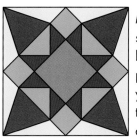

Make a quick sketch of the block and pin scraps of your fabrics to it to use as reference.

Making the block

1 Cut out all the fabric in the required shapes as directed. Cut the E patches with the longest side on the straight grain of the fabric, because otherwise they will stretch and distort the block.

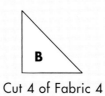

Cut 1 of Fabric 1

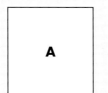

Cut 4 of Fabric 4

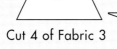

Cut 8 of Fabric 2

Cut 4 of Fabric 3

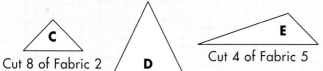

Cut 4 of Fabric 5

Cut 4 of Fabric 4

E

(reversed)
Cut 4 of Fabric 5

2 Join two C patches to each B patch, then add two F patches to two of the pieced units.

 × 2   × 2

3 Join the smaller pieced units to each side of Patch A, then join the larger units to the top and bottom to complete the center square.

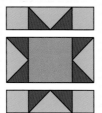

4 Piece the corner units by joining an E and reversed E patch to each D patch.

 × 4

5 With the center square set on point, join a corner unit to each side to complete the block.

Variations

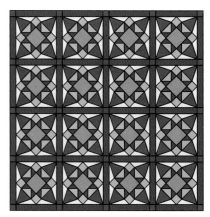

Blocks set with sashings and posts. Notice that the interlocking circles effect still appears.

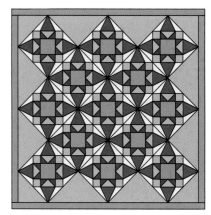

Blocks set on point with plain triangles around the edges.

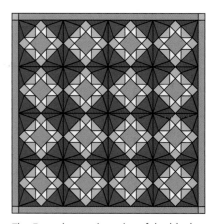

The E patches at the sides of the blocks have been pieced in dark fabric instead of light, emphasizing the kaleidoscope pattern that appears when Dogstooth Violet blocks are repeated.

Brave World

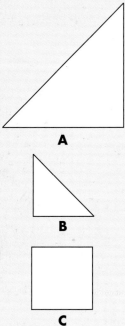
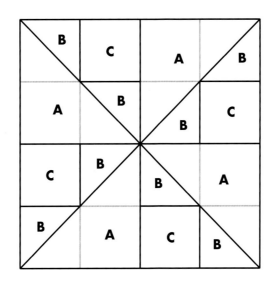

Brave World dates from around the 1940s and is a variation on the familiar pinwheel pattern. Many different forms of pinwheel design are used in patchwork, varying from simple constructions to relatively complex patterns. This one is very easy both to draft and to piece, so it is a perfect block for beginners to make. This example is finished with a plain border.

Drafting

Draft the block on a 4 × 4 grid and make the templates.

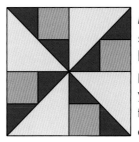

Make a quick sketch of the block and pin scraps of your fabrics to it to use as reference.

Making the block

1 Cut out all the fabric in the required shapes as directed.

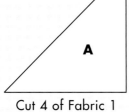

A

Cut 4 of Fabric 1

B

Cut 8 of Fabric 3

C

Cut 4 of Fabric 2

2 Join two B patches to each C patch.

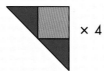 × 4

3 Join an A patch to each of the pieced units.

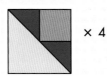 × 4

4 Join the pieced units in pairs, rotating them to form the pattern.

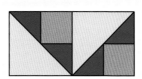

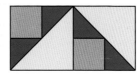

5 Join the rows to complete the block.

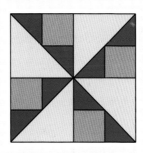

Variations

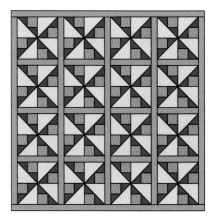

Blocks set with sashings and a plain border.

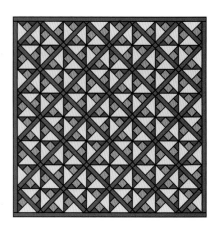

Blocks set on point with half and quarter blocks around the edges. The blocks are emphasized by the dark sashings, posts, and border.

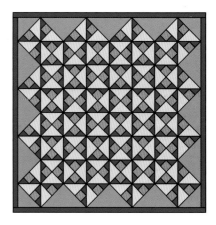

Blocks set on point with plain triangles around the edges.

Windblown Square

SKILL LEVEL ▾

TEMPLATES ▾

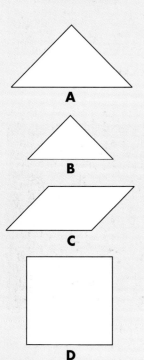

A

B

C

D

FABRICS ▾

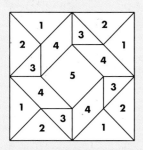

1 MEDIUM
2 DARK
3 MEDIUM LIGHT
4 MEDIUM DARK
5 FEATURE

The arrangement of triangles in this evocatively named block suggests the swirling motion of the wind. The large center square provides an opportunity to use a striking feature fabric—a display of colorful butterflies forms the focal point in this block. The border around this quilt has posts in the same feature fabric as the center square.

Drafting

Draft the block on a 4 × 4 grid and make the templates.

Make a quick sketch of the block and pin scraps of your fabrics to it to use as reference.

Making the block

1 Cut out all the fabric in the required shapes as directed.

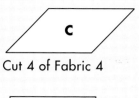

C

Cut 4 of Fabric 4

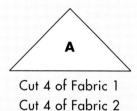

A

Cut 4 of Fabric 1
Cut 4 of Fabric 2

B

Cut 4 of Fabric 3

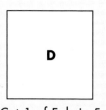

D

Cut 1 of Fabric 5

2 Join pairs of B and C patches together.

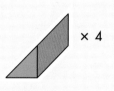 × 4

3 Join a pieced unit to opposite sides of Patch D, then join the two remaining pieced units, setting in the seams (see page 27).

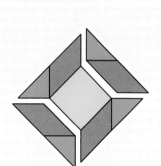

4 Join pairs of A patches to form the corner units.

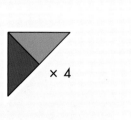 × 4

5 Join the corner units to the center square to complete the block.

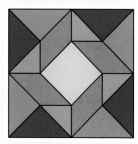

Variations

Blocks set with sashings and posts.

Blocks set on point with sashings and posts. The edges are completed with half and quarter blocks.

Blocks set on point with alternate plain squares and triangles.

Old Maid's Ramble

A

B

C

D

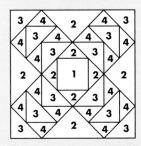

1 *MEDIUM LIGHT*
2 *MEDIUM DARK*
3 *DARK*
4 *LIGHT*

Although this seems to have been its most common name, Old Maid's Ramble was also traditionally known as Crimson Rambler and Vermont. The diagonal emphasis of the pattern produces some interesting subsidiary patterns when blocks are repeated. The quilt shown here is finished with a border and corner posts.

Drafting

Draft the block on an 8 × 8 grid and make the templates.

Make a quick sketch of the block and pin scraps of your fabrics to it to use as reference.

Making the block

1 Cut out all the fabric in the required shapes as directed.

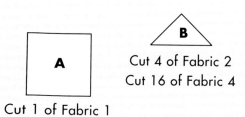

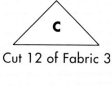
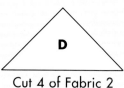

A
Cut 1 of Fabric 1

B
Cut 4 of Fabric 2
Cut 16 of Fabric 4

C
Cut 12 of Fabric 3

D
Cut 4 of Fabric 2

2 Sew a Fabric 2 B patch to each side of Patch A to form the center square.

3 Piece the remaining B and C patches to form the diagonal units.

× 4

4 Add two D patches to two of the diagonal units.

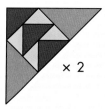

× 2

5 Join the remaining two diagonal units to the center square, then join the three pieced elements to complete the block.

Variations

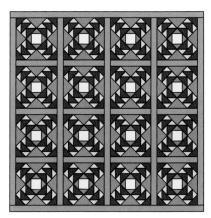

Blocks set with monochrome sashings and border.

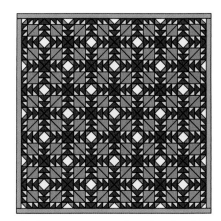

Blocks set on point with a plain border.

Blocks set on point with narrow sashings and posts and a plain border.

West Virginia

SKILL LEVEL ▾

TEMPLATES ▾

A

B

C

FABRICS ▾

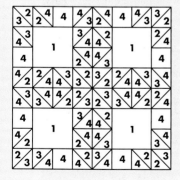

1 *FEATURE*
2 *MEDIUM LIGHT*
3 *MEDIUM DARK*
4 *LIGHT*

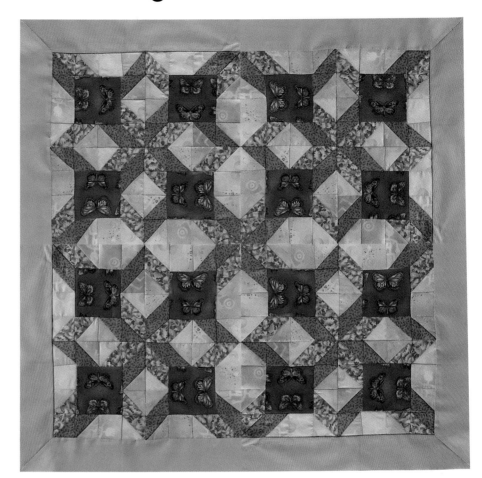

This beautiful block, first published in the 1930s, looks complicated but is actually constructed from four identical units. Repeated blocks form a striking grid pattern, with the larger squares appearing to lie on top of a grid. This example is finished with a mitered border. The whole block is made from squares and half-square triangles, so take great care to piece the patches accurately when handling so many seams.

Drafting

Draft the block on an 8 × 8 grid and make the templates.

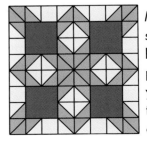

Make a quick sketch of the block and pin scraps of your fabrics to it to use as reference.

Making the block

✂

1 Cut out all the fabric in the required shapes as directed.

A

Cut 4 of Fabric 1

C

Cut 8 of Fabric 4

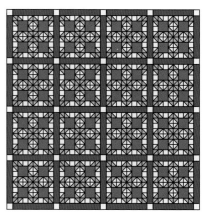

Cut 24 of Fabric 2
Cut 24 of Fabric 3
Cut 32 of Fabric 4

2 Join pairs of B patches together. To speed things up, use the chain piecing method (see page 28).

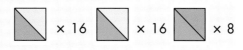 × 16   × 16   × 8

3 Join pieced units and C patches in rows.

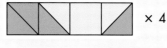 × 4

 × 4

4 Join pairs of the remaining units to opposite sides of each A patch, then add a row of pieced units top and bottom to complete the four quarters of the block.

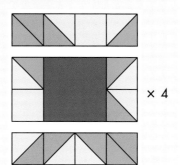 × 4

5 Join pairs of quarter units together, rotating them to form the pattern, then join the rows to complete the block.

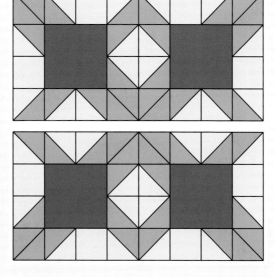

Variations

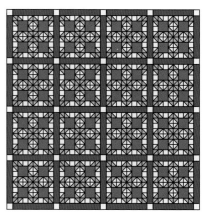

Blocks set with dark sashings and light posts produces a dramatic effect.

Blocks set on point with a plain border.

Blocks set on point with plain triangles around the edges and a matching plain border.

Bridal Path

SKILL LEVEL ▾

TEMPLATES ▾

A

B

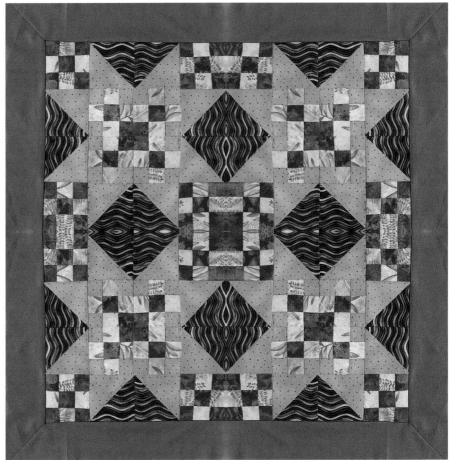

The name of this 1930s block reflects the old tradition whereby a young woman was expected to accumulate 12 quilts in anticipation of her marriage. Although the block looks complicated, only two templates are needed and the checkered squares are very easy to piece. This example is finished with a mitered border.

FABRICS ▾

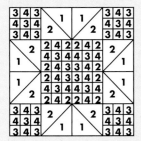

1 DARK
2 MEDIUM LIGHT
3 MEDIUM DARK
4 LIGHT

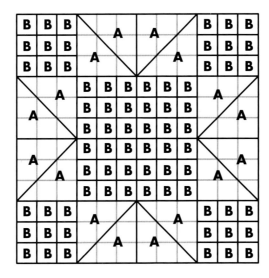

Drafting

Draft the block on a 12 × 12 grid and make the templates.

Make a quick sketch of the block and pin scraps of your fabrics to it to use as reference.

Making the block

✂

1 Cut out all the fabric in the required shapes as directed.

Cut 12 of Fabric 2
Cut 28 of Fabric 3
Cut 32 of Fabric 4

A
Cut 8 of Fabric 1
Cut 8 of Fabric 2

2 Join pairs of A patches together.

× 8

3 Piece the B patches to make the corner and center units.

× 4   × 4

4 Join the pieced units in rows.

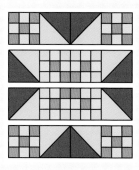

5 Join the rows to complete the block.

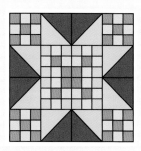

Variations

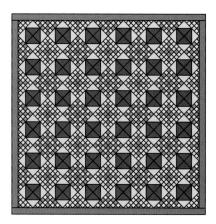

Blocks set on point produce an interesting pattern of diamonds in a variety of pieced designs.

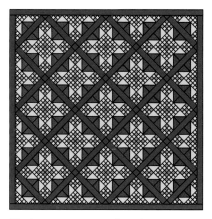

Blocks set on point with sashings, posts, and a plain border.

The use of dark and medium-light colors for the large triangles at the sides of the block have been swapped to emphasize different elements of the design.

SKILL LEVEL ▾

TEMPLATES ▾

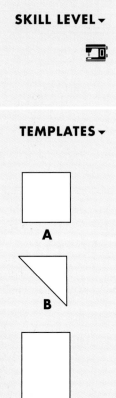

A

B

C

FABRICS ▾

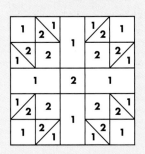

1 *LIGHT*
2 *DARK*

Butterfly at the Crossroads

Butterfly at the Crossroads is another of the many blocks in which the name is an imaginative interpretation of the shapes within it. It is a versatile block that, with some minor amendments, can be transformed into other five-patch blocks. One of these is shown in the variations opposite. This quilt is finished with a border and corner posts.

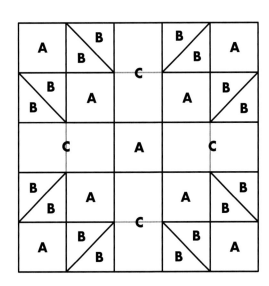

Drafting

Draft the block on a 5 × 5 grid and make the templates.

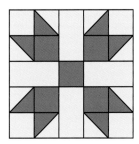

Make a quick sketch of the block and pin scraps of your fabrics to it to use as reference.

Making the block

1 Cut out all the fabric in the required shapes as directed.

 A

 B

 C

Cut 4 of Fabric 1
Cut 5 of Fabric 2

Cut 8 of Fabric 1
Cut 8 of Fabric 2

Cut 4 of Fabric 1

2 Join pairs of B patches together.

× 8

3 Join the pieced elements with A patches to form the corner units.

 × 4

4 Join a corner unit to opposite sides of a C patch to form the top and bottom rows.

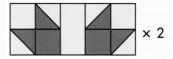 × 2

5 Join the remaining A and C patches together to form the center strip, then join all the elements to complete the block.

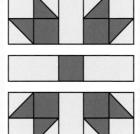

Variations

A third color has been used for the C patches to emphasize the center crosses of each block, and the use of the same fabric for the sashings creates a double grid. The posts are in the same light color as the background.

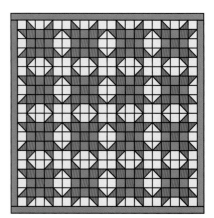

When the C patches are drafted as two squares instead of a rectangle, the pattern becomes another traditional block called Farmer's Daughter.

Handy Andy

SKILL LEVEL ▾

TEMPLATES ▾

A

B

C

D

FABRICS ▾

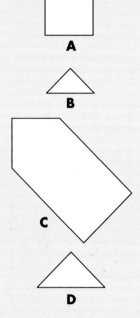

1 LIGHT
2 MEDIUM LIGHT
3 DARK

This is one of several blocks called Handy Andy. Because the large diagonally placed C patches make such a strong graphic impact, you need to choose the fabric for this element of the design carefully. It works well with a striped fabric, as shown in this example, or another strongly patterned fabric. The quilt is finished with a mitered border.

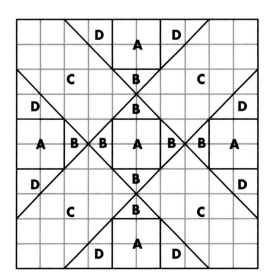

Drafting

Draft the block on a 10 × 10 grid and make the templates.

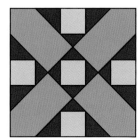

Make a quick sketch of the block and pin scraps of your fabrics to it to use as reference.

Making the block

1 Cut out all the fabric in the required shapes as directed.

A

Cut 5 of Fabric 2

B

Cut 8 of Fabric 3

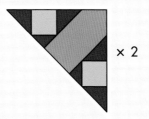

C

Cut 4 of Fabric 1

D

Cut 8 of Fabric 3

2 Join two D patches, one A patch, and one B patch together.

× 4

3 Join a pieced unit to opposite sides of a C patch to form the corner elements.

× 2

4 Join a B patch to each side of the remaining A patch to form the center square.

5 Join the remaining C patches to opposite sides of the center square, then join all the elements to complete the block.

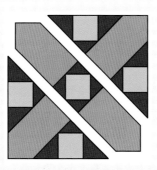

Variations

When blocks are set with sashings and posts, the strong underlying lattice is broken up and appears less dominant.

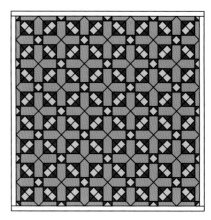

Blocks set on point, producing a completely different effect, with a pattern of crosses appearing over an underlying lattice.

Crazy House

SKILL LEVEL ▾

TEMPLATES ▾

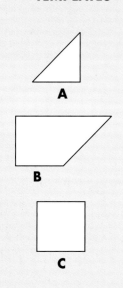

A

B

C

FABRICS ▾

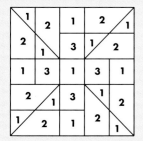

1 *LIGHT*
2 *MEDIUM*
3 *DARK*

Crazy House was first published in 1928—but without an explanation for the name. Composed of four identical corner units joined by a built-in grid of sashings, it is a very easy block to piece, though you will need to take care when making the corner units to ensure that the seams meet up accurately. This example is finished with a border and corner posts.

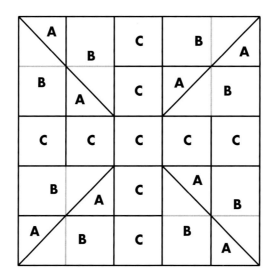

Drafting

Draft the block on a 5 × 5 grid and make the templates.

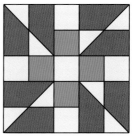

Make a quick sketch of the block and pin scraps of your fabrics to it to use as reference.

Making the block

1 Cut out all the fabric in the required shapes as directed.

 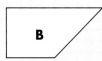

Cut 8 of Fabric 1   Cut 8 of Fabric 2   Cut 5 of Fabric 1
Cut 4 of Fabric 3

2 Join pairs of A and B patches together.

 × 8

3 Join pairs of pieced elements to form the corner units.

 × 4

4 Join the C patches together.

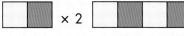 × 2   × 1

5 Join the pieced elements in rows, rotating the corner units to form the pattern, then join the rows to complete the block.

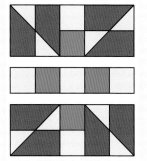

Variations

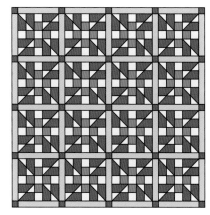

Blocks set with sashings and posts.

Blocks set on point with a plain border. The quilt is completed with half and quarter blocks around the edges.

Blocks set on point with alternate plain squares and triangles.

Jack in the Box

SKILL LEVEL ▾

TEMPLATES ▾

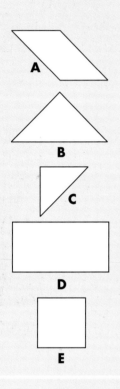

A

B

C

D

E

FABRICS ▾

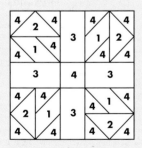

1 MEDIUM
2 LIGHT
3 MEDIUM LIGHT
4 DARK

Jack in the Box is also known as Whirligig, which is an apt description of the pattern. Once again, this five-patch pattern has built-in sashings and posts that join up when the blocks are repeated to give the familiar lattice effect. This example is finished with a border and corner posts.

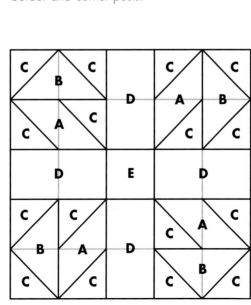

Drafting

Draft the block on a 5 × 5 grid and make the templates.

Make a quick sketch of the block and pin scraps of your fabrics to it to use as reference.

Making the block

1 Cut out all the fabric in the required shapes as directed.

Cut 4 of Fabric 1

Cut 4 of Fabric 2

Cut 16 of Fabric 4

D

Cut 4 of Fabric 3

E

Cut 1 of Fabric 4

2 Join two C patches to each A patch, and two C patches to each B patch.

 × 4   × 4

3 Join the two pieced units to make the corner squares.

 × 4

4 Join a corner unit to opposite sides of a D patch to make the top and bottom rows, rotating the units to form the pattern.

 × 2

5 Join the remaining D and E patches to make the center strip, then join all the elements to complete the block.

Variations

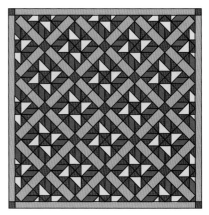

Blocks set on point with a border and corner posts in the same fabric as the built-in sashings of the blocks.

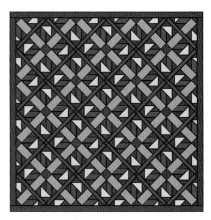

Blocks set on point with narrow sashings and posts.

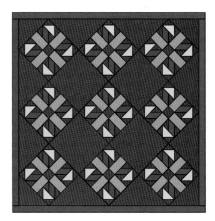

Blocks set on point with alternating plain squares and triangles in the same dark fabric as that used in the background of the pieced blocks.

Single Wedding Ring

SKILL LEVEL ▾

TEMPLATES ▾

A

B

This block is a good candidate for a scrap quilt. If you use the same fabric for the ring in the center—perhaps a feature or very bright fabric—you can piece the remaining patches from a mixture of fabrics, provided you choose ones with a good light/dark contrast. This quilt is finished with a border and corner posts. Only two templates are needed, so this is a really easy block to piece.

FABRICS ▾

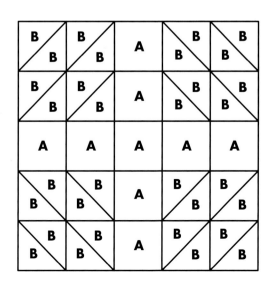

1 *MEDIUM*
2 *DARK*
3 *LIGHT*

Drafting

Draft the block on a 5 × 5 grid and make the templates.

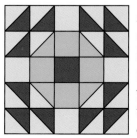

Make a quick sketch of the block and pin scraps of your fabrics to it to use as reference.

Making the block

1 Cut out all the fabric in the required shapes as directed.

Cut 4 of Fabric 1
Cut 1 of Fabric 2
Cut 4 of Fabric 3

Cut 4 of Fabric 1
Cut 12 of Fabric 2
Cut 16 of Fabric 3

2 Join pairs of B patches together.

 × 12   × 4

3 Lay out all the pieced units and squares and join them into five rows.

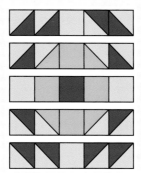

4 Join the rows to complete the block.

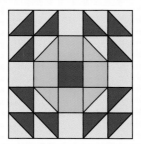

Variations

The corner patches of the block are pieced in a contrasting color, creating additional focal points in the quilt.

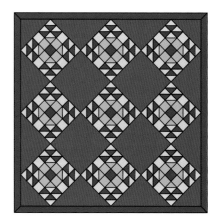

Blocks set on point with a plain border.

Blocks set on point with alternate plain squares and triangles.

Domino

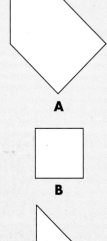

A

B

C

The diagonally placed A patches make an interesting grid pattern across the surface of the quilt when repeated blocks are placed side by side. As you will see from the variations opposite, interesting effects occur when some of the patches are recolored. This example is finished with a plain border.

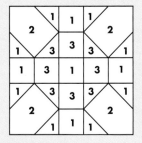

1 *LIGHT*
2 *DARK*
3 *MEDIUM*

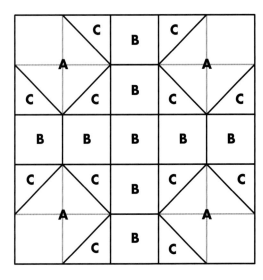

Drafting

Draft the block on a 5 × 5 grid and make the templates.

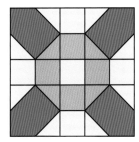

Make a quick sketch of the block and pin scraps of your fabrics to it to use as reference.

Making the block

1 Cut out all the fabric in the required shapes as directed.

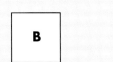

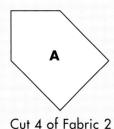

Cut 5 of Fabric 1
Cut 4 of Fabric 3

Cut 8 of Fabric 1
Cut 4 of Fabric 3

Cut 4 of Fabric 2

2 Join A and C patches together to form the corner units.

 × 4

3 Join pairs of B patches together.

 × 2

4 Join the pieced units to form the top and bottom rows of the block.

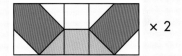 × 2

5 Join the remaining B patches together to form the central strip, then join all the rows to complete the block.

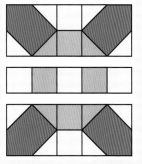

Variations

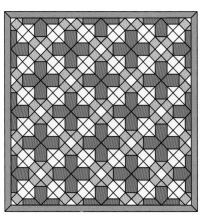

When blocks are set on point, lines of crosses appear as one of the main elements of the pattern.

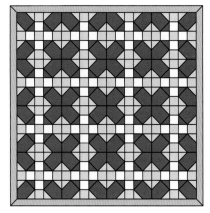

Using the same color for the A and inner C patches emphasizes the lattice effect.

Grape Basket

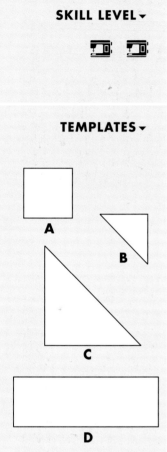
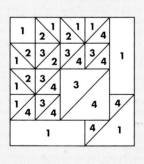
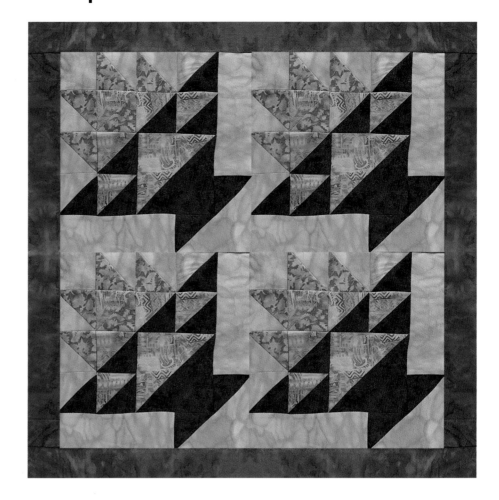

Pieced baskets are a popular traditional patchwork theme, and there are many variations. Because they are not symmetrical, the repeated blocks make several interesting patterns. This example is finished with a plain border and uses a light background fabric, but you would get equally pleasing effects by reversing the light/dark contrasts in the block, as shown in the variations opposite.

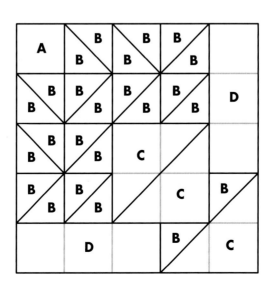

Drafting

Draft the block on a 5 × 5 grid and make the templates.

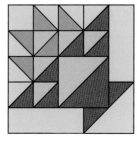

Make a quick sketch of the block and pin scraps of your fabrics to it to use as reference.

Making the block

1 Cut out all the fabric in the required shapes as directed.

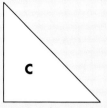

A

Cut 1 of Fabric 1

B

Cut 6 of Fabric 1
Cut 5 of Fabric 2
Cut 5 of Fabric 3
Cut 8 of Fabric 4

C

Cut 1 of Fabric 1
Cut 1 of Fabric 3
Cut 1 of Fabric 4

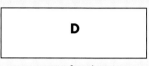

Cut 2 of Fabric 1

2 Piece pairs of B patches together. Use the chain piecing method if you are making several blocks (see page 28).

× 4   × 2

× 4   × 1

3 Use the pieced triangles and Patch A to form three units.

4 Join the Fabric 3 C and Fabric 4 C patches together to create a fourth unit, then join all four units to form the main body of the basket.

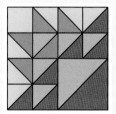

5 Join a B patch to each D patch and join them to the sides of the basket. Add the remaining C patch to the corner to complete the block.

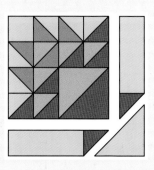

Variations

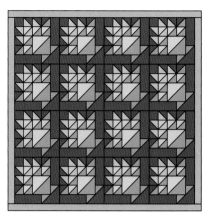

Dark background fabric has been used instead of a light color, producing an equally effective result.

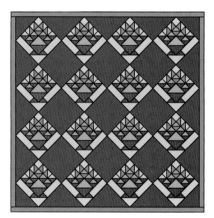

Blocks set on point with alternating plain squares and triangles.

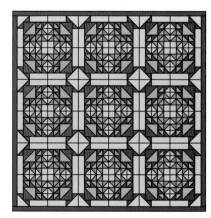

Thirty-six blocks set in groups of four. The blocks in each group are rotated so that the A patches meet in the center.

Grandmother's Cross

SKILL LEVEL ▾

TEMPLATES ▾

A

B

C

This is a slight variation on a block first published in the 1930s and also known as Southern Cross. It is an easy block to construct because only four units need to be pieced; the rest of the patches are squares. This quilt is finished with a plain border.

FABRICS ▾

4	1	1/2	1	1	4
1	3	2	3	1
2/1	2	2	2	2/1
1	3	2	3	1
4	1	2/1	1	4

1 MEDIUM
2 MEDIUM DARK
3 LIGHT
4 DARK

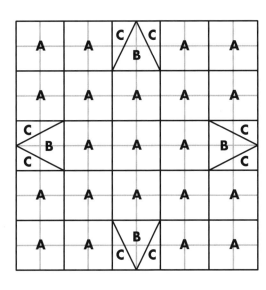

Drafting

Draft the block on a 10 × 10 grid and make the templates.

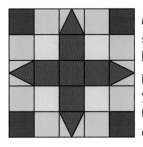

Make a quick sketch of the block and pin scraps of your fabrics to it to use as reference.

Making the block

1 Cut out all the fabric in the required shapes as directed.

B
Cut 4 of Fabric 2

C
Cut 4 of Fabric 1

C (reversed)
Cut 4 of Fabric 1

A
Cut 8 of Fabric 1
Cut 5 of Fabric 2
Cut 4 of Fabric 3
Cut 4 of Fabric 4

2 Join a C and reversed C patch to each B patch.

 × 4

3 Lay out all the squares and pieced units and join them into five rows.

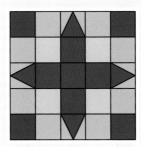

4 Join the rows to complete the block.

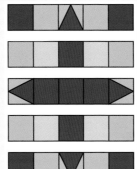

Variations

Blocks set with sashings and posts.

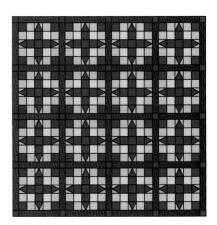

Blocks set with dark sashings produces a more dramatic effect.

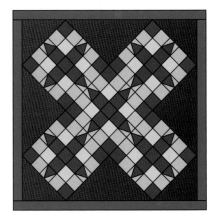

Five blocks set on point on a dark background makes a striking wall quilt.

Queen Charlotte's Crown

SKILL LEVEL ▾

TEMPLATES ▾

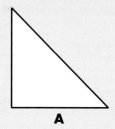

A

B

C

FABRICS ▾

1 *MEDIUM LIGHT*
2 *MEDIUM DARK*
3 *DARK*

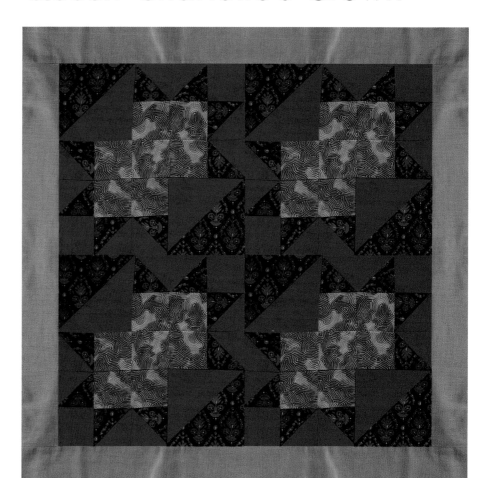

Queen Charlotte was the wife of England's George III and, therefore, the last queen of America. Charlotte, North Carolina, is named in her honor, and so is this block, although after 1770 it was renamed Indian Meadow. The center patches merge to form an interesting shape, so it is important to choose a striking fabric for them. The quilt is finished here with a plain border.

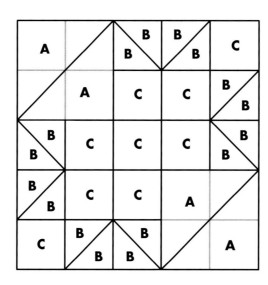

Drafting

Draft the block on a 5 × 5 grid and make the templates.

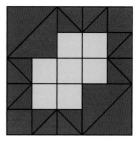

Make a quick sketch of the block and pin scraps of your fabrics to it to use as reference.

Making the block

1 Cut out all the fabric in the required shapes as directed.

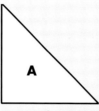

Cut 8 of Fabric 2	Cut 7 of Fabric 1	Cut 2 of Fabric 2
Cut 8 of Fabric 3	Cut 2 of Fabric 2	Cut 2 of Fabric 3

2 Join pairs of A patches and pairs of B patches together.

 × 2   × 8

3 Join pieced units and C patches to form the top and bottom sections of the block.

 × 2

4 Join the remaining C patches and pieced units to form the center strip.

5 Lay out the three sections, rotating the lower element, then join them to complete the block.

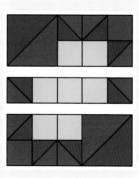

Variations

By rotating alternate blocks 90 degrees, a very different pattern is revealed.

Blocks set on point with plain triangles around the edges.

Leap Frog

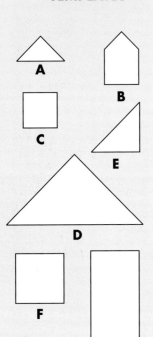
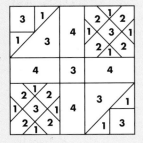

Leap Frog probably dates from around the turn of the twentieth century. It is an unusual block in that it has two completely different pieced units on opposite sides. This, added to the built-in sashings, results in complex patterns when blocks are repeated. Do not be put off by the number of templates needed—neither of the two sections is difficult to piece. This example is finished with a border and corner posts.

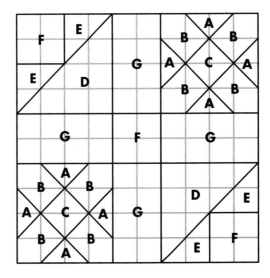

Drafting

Draft the block on a 10 × 10 grid and make the templates.

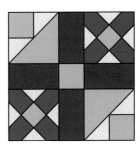

Make a quick sketch of the block and pin scraps of your fabrics to it to use as reference.

Making the block

1 Cut out all the fabric in the required shapes as directed.

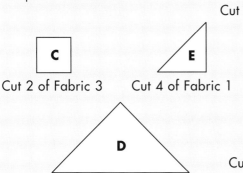

Cut 8 of Fabric 1

Cut 8 of Fabric 2

C Cut 2 of Fabric 3

E Cut 4 of Fabric 1

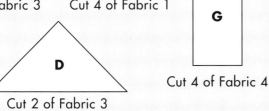

D Cut 2 of Fabric 3

G Cut 4 of Fabric 4

F Cut 3 of Fabric 3

2 Join A, B, and C patches into units.

× 4   × 2

3 Join the pieced units to make two corner squares.

× 2

4 Join D, E, and F patches to form the remaining corner squares.

× 2

5 Join the corner squares and remaining patches into rows, then join the rows to complete the block.

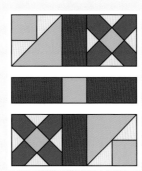

Variations

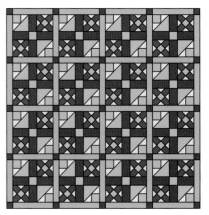

Blocks set with sashings and posts creates the illusion that the underlying pattern is being seen through two layers.

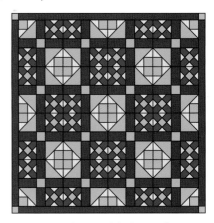

By rotating alternate blocks 90 degrees, the quilt appears to have been made from two different blocks.

The corner units have been pieced in different colors. When the rotated blocks are set with sashings and posts, the blue squares and lilac crosses appear to radiate out from under the dark grid placed over them.

Goose Tracks

SKILL LEVEL ▾

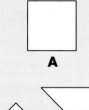

TEMPLATES ▾

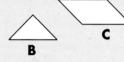

A

B

C

D

E

FABRICS ▾

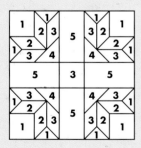

1 *MEDIUM LIGHT*
2 *MEDIUM DARK*
3 *DARK*
4 *MEDIUM*
5 *LIGHT*

Goose Tracks is another five-patch pattern with a center sashing that produces interesting effects when blocks are repeated—the "petal" shapes in each corner join to make what appears to be a completely different block set with sashings and posts. Four Goose Tracks blocks joined in this way make a beautiful wall quilt. This example is finished with a plain border.

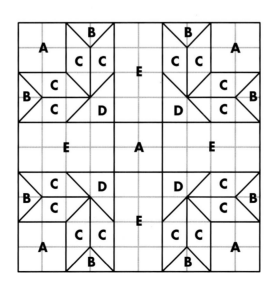

Drafting

Draft the block on a 10 × 10 grid and make the templates.

Make a quick sketch of the block and pin scraps of your fabrics to it to use as reference.

Making the block

1 Cut out all the fabric in the required shapes as directed.

A

Cut 4 of Fabric 1
Cut 1 of Fabric 3

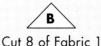

B

Cut 8 of Fabric 1

D

Cut 4 of Fabric 4

E

Cut 4 of Fabric 5

C

Cut 4 of Fabric 2
Cut 4 of Fabric 3

C
(reversed)

Cut 4 of Fabric 2
Cut 4 of Fabric 3

2 Join two C and two reversed C patches together, then add a D patch to the corner.

 × 4

3 Complete the corners units by adding one A and two B patches, setting in the seams (see page 27).

 × 4

4 Join a corner unit to opposite sides of an E patch to make the top and bottom rows, rotating the units to form the pattern.

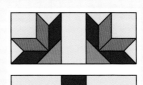 × 2

5 Join the remaining A and E patches to form the center strip. Lay out the three elements and join the rows to complete the block.

Variations

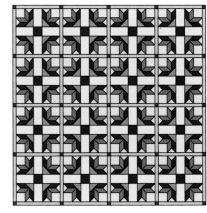

Blocks set with narrow sashings, border, and posts.

Blocks set on point with a mitered border.

Blocks set on point with plain triangles around the edges and a matching plain border.

Wild Rose and Square

SKILL LEVEL ▾

TEMPLATES ▾

A

B

C

FABRICS ▾

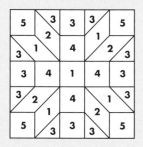

1 *MEDIUM*
2 *MEDIUM LIGHT*
3 *MEDIUM DARK*
4 *LIGHT*
5 *DARK*

When the B patches in each corner unit are pieced in different tones of the same color, they produce a three-dimensional effect that is emphasized if dark squares are set into the corners. Apart from the need to set in the seams for the corner squares, the block is straightforward to piece. This quilt is finished with a mitered border.

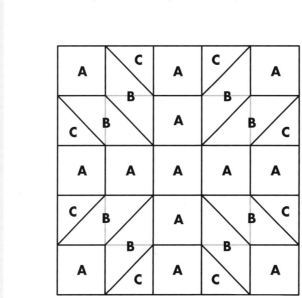

Drafting

Draft the block on a 5 × 5 grid and make the templates.

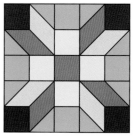

Make a quick sketch of the block and pin scraps of your fabrics to it to use as reference.

Making the block

1 Cut out all the fabric in the required shapes as directed.

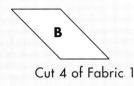

C

Cut 8 of Fabric 3

A

Cut 1 of Fabric 1
Cut 4 of Fabric 3
Cut 4 of Fabric 4
Cut 4 of Fabric 5

B

Cut 4 of Fabric 1

B

(reversed)
Cut 4 of Fabric 2

2 Join pairs of B and reversed B patches together, then add a Fabric 5 A patch in the corner, setting in the seams (see page 27).

 × 4

3 Add pairs of C patches to complete the corner units.

 × 4

4 Join the remaining A patches together.

× 2

× 1

5 Lay out the pieced elements and join them in rows, rotating the corner units to form the pattern. Join the rows to complete the block.

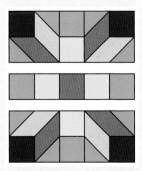

Variations

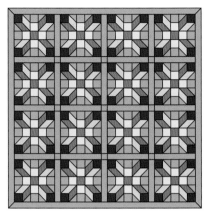

Blocks set with sashings, posts, and a mitered border, all in the same color.

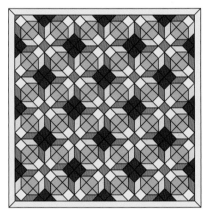

Blocks set on point with a mitered border.

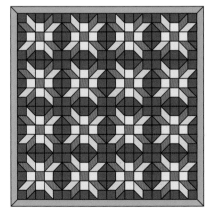

All of the patches around the outside edges of the blocks have been pieced in a single color to emphasize the wild rose design.

Crazy Ann

SKILL LEVEL ▾

TEMPLATES ▾

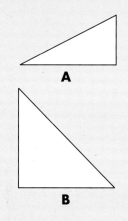

A

B

C   D

FABRICS ▾

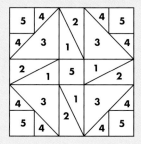

1 *DARK*
2 *MEDIUM LIGHT*
3 *MEDIUM*
4 *LIGHT*
5 *MEDIUM*

This interesting block has built-in movement; its other names are Follow the Leader and the descriptive Twist and Turn. Repeated blocks produce the effect of a pieced grid, so when the blocks are joined with sashings, the pattern looks even more complex and the underlying design is seen through layers. This example is finished with a border and corner posts.

Drafting

Draft the block on a 5 × 5 grid and make the templates.

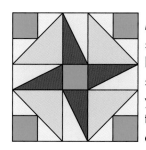

Make a quick sketch of the block and pin scraps of your fabrics to it to use as reference.

Making the block

✂

1 Cut out all the fabric in the required shapes as directed.

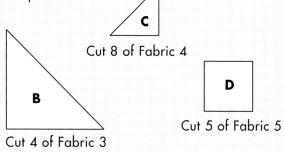

C

Cut 8 of Fabric 4

A

Cut 4 of Fabric 1
Cut 4 of Fabric 2

B

Cut 4 of Fabric 3

D

Cut 5 of Fabric 5

2 Join B, C, and D patches to form the corner units.

 × 4

3 Join pairs of A patches together.

 × 4

4 Join the pieced elements to form the top and bottom rows, rotating the corner units to form the pattern.

 × 2

5 Join the remaining pieced units and D patch to form the center strip. Lay out the elements and join the rows to complete the block.

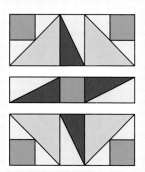

Variations

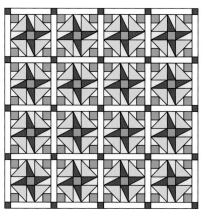

When blocks are set with sashings and posts, a pronounced layered effect is achieved.

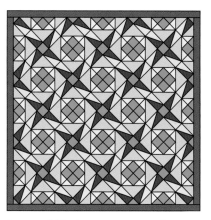

Repeated blocks set on point with a plain border. The twisted design of the built-in sashings creates a prominent diagonal grid that frames three interlocking squares.

SKILL LEVEL ▾

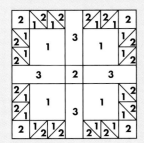

TEMPLATES ▾

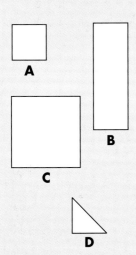

FABRICS ▾

1 *DARK*
2 *LIGHT*
3 *MEDIUM*

Bear's Paw

Like many blocks, this one has had different names in different places and at different times. For instance, it was called Bear's Paw in Pennsylvania and Ohio in 1850, but the Quakers of Philadelphia called it Hand of Friendship. Several blocks go under the name of Bear's Paw; this seven-patch version is very simple to piece but has great design potential. It is set here with a border and posts to echo the interior sashings.

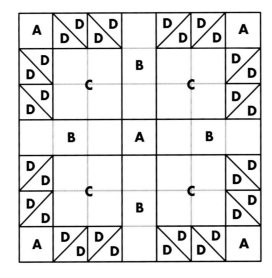

Drafting

Draft the block on a 7 × 7 grid and make the templates.

Make a quick sketch of the block and pin scraps of your fabrics to it to use as reference.

Making the block

✂

1 Cut out all the fabric in the required shapes as directed.

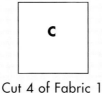

C

Cut 4 of Fabric 1

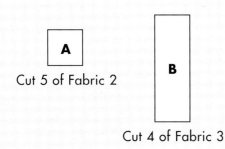

A

Cut 5 of Fabric 2

B

Cut 4 of Fabric 3

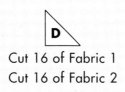

D

Cut 16 of Fabric 1
Cut 16 of Fabric 2

2 Join pairs of D patches together. Use the chain piecing method if you are making several blocks (see page 28).

 × 16

3 Join the pieced elements with A and C patches to form the corner units.

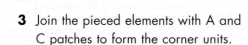 × 4

4 Join a corner unit to opposite sides of a B patch to form the top and bottom rows, rotating the units to form the pattern.

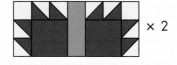 × 2

5 Join the remaining A and B patches to form the center strip. Lay out the three elements and join the rows to complete the block.

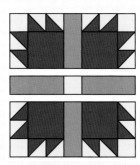

Variations

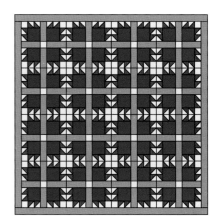

A different color has been used for the C patches in each block, emphasizing the pattern of squares beneath the grid formed by the central crosses of the blocks.

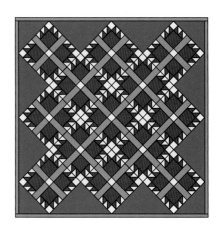

Thirteen blocks set on point with plain triangles around the edges. This quilt does not need a border but can be finished with bound edges.

Greek Cross

SKILL LEVEL ▾

TEMPLATES ▾

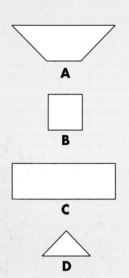

FABRICS ▾

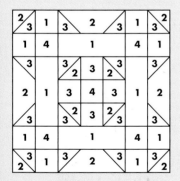

1 MEDIUM DARK
2 LIGHT
3 MEDIUM LIGHT
4 DARK

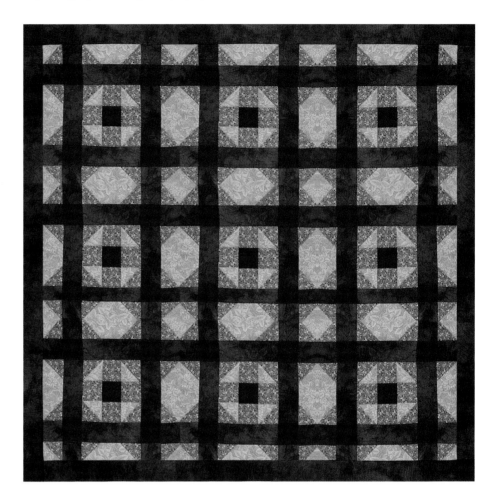

This block looks deceptively complex but is easily achieved if you join the seams accurately. Repeated blocks reveal crosses and squares lying beneath a grid, while the light patches around the edges join to form squares and long hexagons. The border and corner posts of this quilt match the sashings and posts within the block.

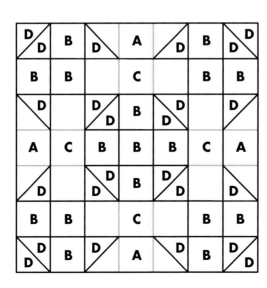

Drafting

Draft the block on a 7 × 7 grid and make the templates.

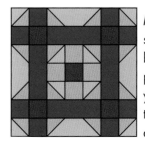

Make a quick sketch of the block and pin scraps of your fabrics to it to use as reference.

Making the block

1 Cut out all the fabric in the required shapes as directed.

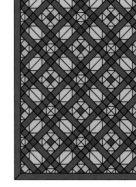

B

Cut 8 of Fabric 1
Cut 4 of Fabric 3
Cut 5 of Fabric 4

A

Cut 4 of Fabric 2

C

Cut 4 of Fabric 1

D

Cut 8 of Fabric 2
Cut 16 of Fabric 3

2 Join pairs of Fabric 3 D patches to each A patch, then join the remaining D patches together in pairs.

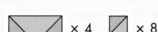 × 4   × 8

3 Join five B patches and four pieced D units to form the center square.

4 Piece B and C patches together to form the horizontal sashes.

 × 2

5 Join the pieced units and remaining patches in rows, then join the rows to complete the block.

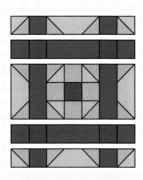

Variations

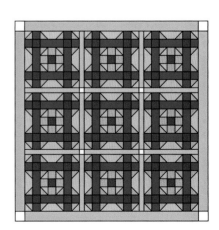

Blocks set on point with a mitered border in the same color as the built-in sashings.

Nine blocks set on point with alternate plain squares and triangles and a plain border.

Blocks set with narrow sashings and a wide border in a contrasting color to emphasize the layered effect.

SKILL LEVEL ▾

TEMPLATES ▾

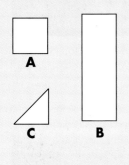

A

B

C

D

FABRICS ▾

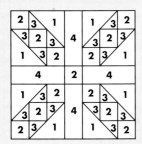

1 DARK
2 MEDIUM DARK
3 LIGHT
4 MEDIUM LIGHT

Buffalo Ridge Quilt

This interesting block appears to be fairly modern. It was first published under this name in 1972, then again as Country Roads in 1979. Repeated blocks produce the effect of an intricately pieced diagonal lattice lying beneath a grid. This example is finished with a pieced border of sashings and posts in the same fabrics as those used in the blocks.

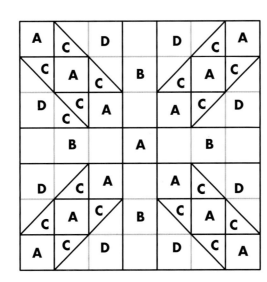

Drafting

Draft the block on a 7 × 7 grid and make the templates.

Make a quick sketch of the block and pin scraps of your fabrics to it to use as reference.

Making the block

1 Cut out all the fabric in the required shapes as directed.

Cut 13 of Fabric 2

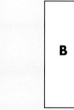
Cut 16 of Fabric 3

B
Cut 4 of Fabric 4

D
Cut 8 of Fabric 1

2 Piece A and C patches together.

× 8   × 4

3 Join the pieced units to form the diagonal lattice.

× 4

4 Add pairs of D patches to each lattice element to form the corner units.

× 4

5 Join the corner units and remaining patches in rows, then join the rows to complete the block.

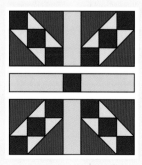

Variations

Blocks set on point with half and quarter blocks around the edges and a plain border.

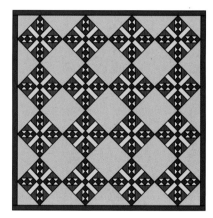

Blocks set on point with alternate plain squares and triangles.

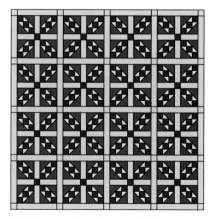

Blocks set with sashings and posts to create yet another layer.

Girl's Joy

SKILL LEVEL ▾

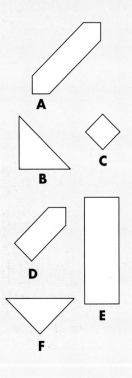

TEMPLATES ▾

A

B

C

D

E

F

FABRICS ▾

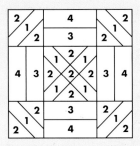

1 MEDIUM DARK
2 MEDIUM LIGHT
3 LIGHT
4 MEDIUM

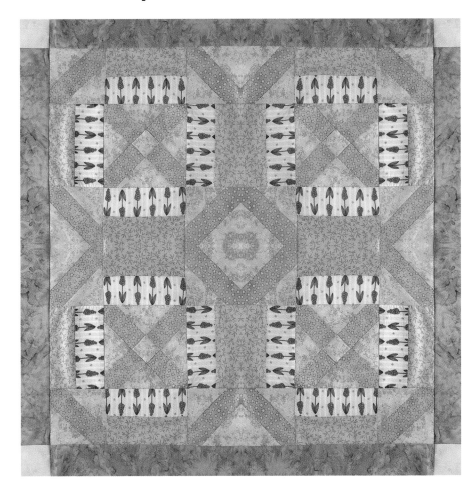

This charming block, dating from around 1898, is also known as Maiden's Delight. This example, finished with a border and corner posts, has been pieced in pretty pastel colors to create a light, summery look. The piecing is straightforward, but take care with the center square, cutting the F patch triangles with the long edges on the straight grain of the fabric. Take care also not to confuse the B and F triangles.

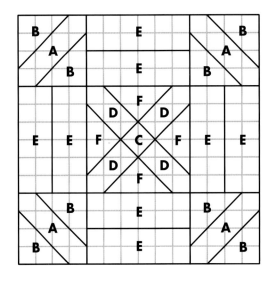

Drafting

Draft the block on a 14 × 14 grid and make the templates.

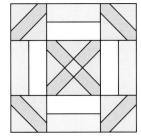

Make a quick sketch of the block and pin scraps of your fabrics to it to use as reference.

Making the block

1 Cut out all the fabric in the required shapes as directed.

A

Cut 4 of Fabric 1

B

Cut 8 of Fabric 2

D

Cut 4 of Fabric 1

E

Cut 4 of Fabric 3
Cut 4 of Fabric 4

C

Cut 1 of Fabric 2

F

Cut 4 of Fabric 2

2 Join two B patches to each A patch, then join pairs of E patches together.

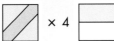 × 4  × 4

3 Join the C, D, and F patches together to form the center square elements.

 × 2 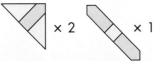 × 1

4 Piece the center square elements together.

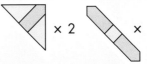

5 Lay out and join the pieced units in rows, then join the rows to complete the block.

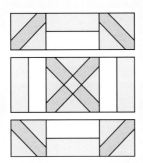

Variations

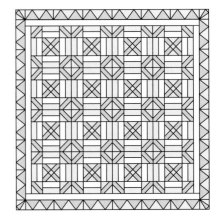

This example is finished with a narrow plain border surrounded by a pieced Dogstooth border.

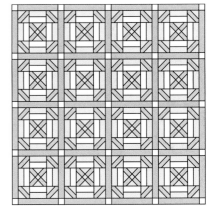

Blocks set with a border, sashings, and posts.

Blocks set on point with a plain border.

Dove at the Window

TEMPLATES ▾

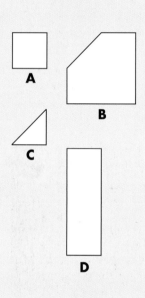

Dove at the Window recalls a time when every barn had round holes cut in the gable for the comfort and convenience of doves. It is another seven-patch block with an interior sashing, so when blocks are repeated in the quilt top the effect is satisfyingly complex. It is often best to finish the edges of such quilts by echoing the sashings and posts within the block, as in this example.

FABRICS ▾

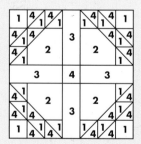

1 DARK
2 MEDIUM LIGHT
3 MEDIUM DARK
4 LIGHT

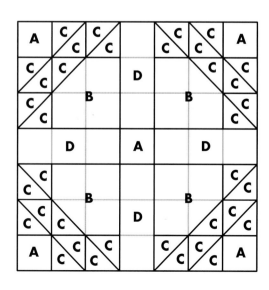

Drafting

Draft the block on a 7 × 7 grid and make the templates.

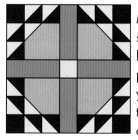

Make a quick sketch of the block and pin scraps of your fabrics to it to use as reference.

Making the block

1 Cut out all the fabric in the required shapes as directed.

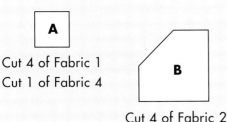

A

Cut 4 of Fabric 1
Cut 1 of Fabric 4

B

Cut 4 of Fabric 2

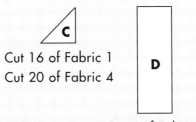

C

Cut 16 of Fabric 1
Cut 20 of Fabric 4

D

Cut 4 of Fabric 3

2 Piece one A and seven C patches together, then piece pairs of C patches to each B patch.

3 Join the pieced units to form the corner squares.

 × 4

4 Join a corner unit to opposite sides of a D patch to form the top and bottom rows, rotating the units to form the pattern.

 × 2

5 Join the remaining A and D patches to form the center strip. Lay out the three elements and join the rows to complete the block.

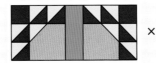

Variations

A narrow black border within the wide yellow border adds definition to the main field of the quilt top. The yellow border echoes the color in the blocks.

Blocks set on point with plain triangles around the edges.

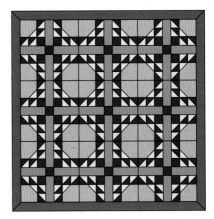

The corner units have been rotated so that the A patches meet in the center of the block to produce a striking diamond design.

Stonemason's Puzzle

SKILL LEVEL ▾

TEMPLATES ▾

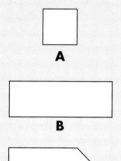

A

B

C

D

FABRICS ▾

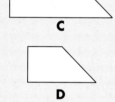

1 DARK
2 MEDIUM LIGHT
3 MEDIUM DARK
4 LIGHT

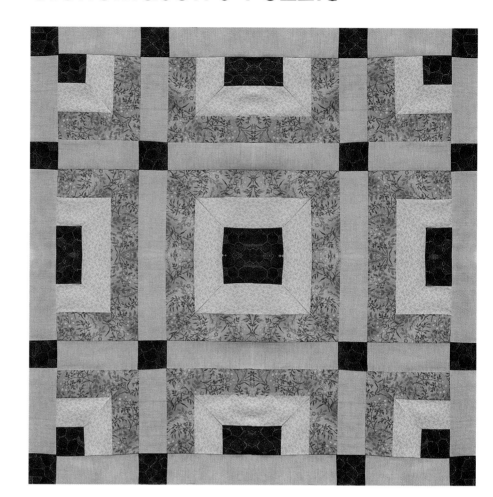

The pattern of this quilt, finished here with a border and posts, dates from the 1920s. As with other designs that have built-in sashings, when blocks are repeated the effect is of a completely different pieced block that has been set with sashings and posts. The pattern becomes even more complex if you set the blocks with additional sashings and posts.

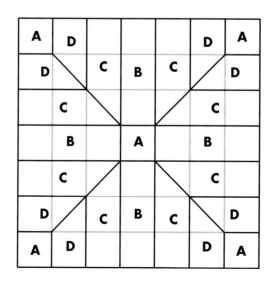

Drafting

Draft the block on a 7 × 7 grid and make the templates.

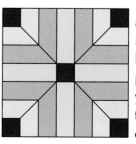

Make a quick sketch of the block and pin scraps of your fabrics to it to use as reference.

Making the block

✂

1 Cut out all the fabric in the required shapes as directed.

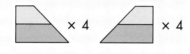

C
Cut 4 of Fabric 3

D
Cut 4 of Fabric 4

B
Cut 4 of Fabric 2

C (reversed)
Cut 4 of Fabric 3

D
(reversed)
Cut 4 of Fabric 4

A
Cut 5 of Fabric 1

2 Join pairs of C and D patches together, and pairs of reversed C and reversed D patches together.

 × 4 × 4

3 Join pairs of pieced units together, then add an A patch to each pair, setting in the seams (see page 27), to form the corner elements.

× 4

4 Sew two B patches to the remaining A patch to form the center strip.

5 Join the corner units and remaining B patches to form the top and bottom rows, then join the rows to complete the block.

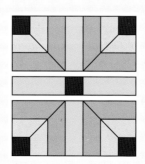

Variations

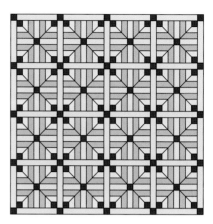

Blocks set with sashings, border, and posts in the same color scheme as the built-in sashings of the block.

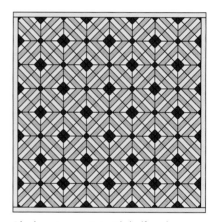

Blocks set on point with half and quarter blocks around the edges and a plain border.

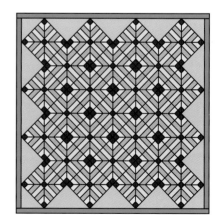

Blocks set on point with plain triangles around the edges and a plain border.

Seven-patch Flower

SKILL LEVEL ▾

TEMPLATES ▾

A

B

C

FABRICS ▾

1 LIGHT
2 MEDIUM LIGHT
3 MEDIUM
4 DARK
5 MEDIUM DARK

This quilt, finished with a mitered border, looks a lot more complicated than it is, with the C patch rectangles appearing to join together as sashings when blocks are repeated. With only three templates, this is not a difficult block to piece, but look carefully to see how the corner units are constructed.

Drafting

Draft the block on a 7 × 7 grid and make the templates.

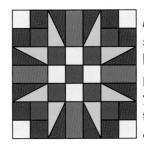

Make a quick sketch of the block and pin scraps of your fabrics to it to use as reference.

Making the block

1 Cut out all the fabric in the required shapes as directed.

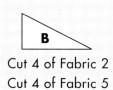

A

Cut 8 of Fabric 1
Cut 9 of Fabric 3
Cut 8 of Fabric 5

B

Cut 4 of Fabric 2
Cut 4 of Fabric 5

B

(reversed)
Cut 4 of Fabric 2
Cut 4 of Fabric 5

C

Cut 4 of Fabric 4

2 Piece four A patches together. Join pairs of B patches, then add a Fabric 3 A patch to them. Join pairs of reversed B patches together.

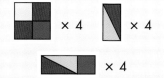

3 Join the pieced elements to form the corner units.

 × 4

4 Piece the remaining A and C patches to form the internal sashings.

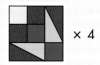 × 2

× 1

5 Join the pieced units in rows, then join the rows to complete the block.

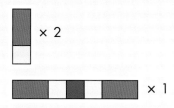

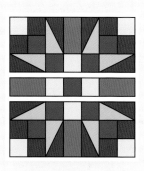

Variations

Blocks set with sashings, border, and posts.

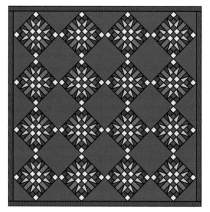

Blocks set on point with half and quarter blocks around the edges and a mitered border.

Blocks set on point with alternate plain squares and triangles in a dark color that helps to highlight the star grid of the main block design.

Stepping Stones

SKILL LEVEL ▾

TEMPLATES ▾

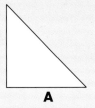

A

B

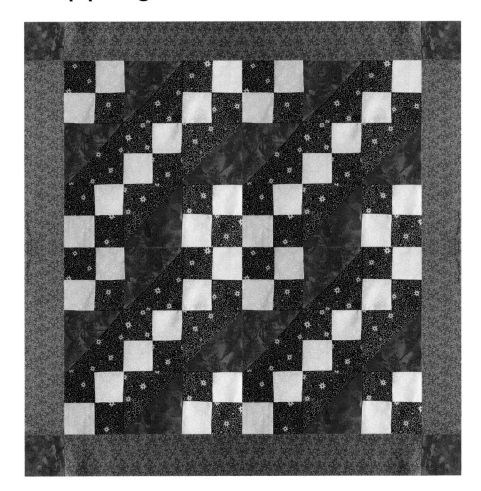

This is but one of many variations on the very old Jacob's Ladder block. The striking graphic impact depends on the use of fabrics with a strong light/dark contrast, which results in a series of stripes running across the quilt. Interesting patterns emerge when repeated blocks are rotated, making this an excellent scrap quilt, provided the color contrasts are strong. This quilt is finished with a border and corner posts.

FABRICS ▾

1 *DARK*
2 *LIGHT*
3 *MEDIUM*

B	B	A		B	B
B	B		A	B	B
A		B	B		A
	A	B	B		A
B	B	A		B	B
B	B		A	B	B

Drafting

Draft the block on a 6 × 6 grid and make the templates.

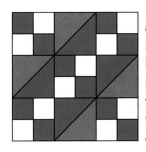

Make a quick sketch of the block and pin scraps of your fabrics to it to use as reference.

Making the block

1 Cut out all the fabric in the required shapes as directed.

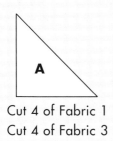

Cut 4 of Fabric 1
Cut 4 of Fabric 3

B

Cut 10 of Fabric 1
Cut 10 of Fabric 2

2 Join pairs of A patches together.

 × 4

3 Join the B patches together.

 × 5

4 Join the pieced units in rows.

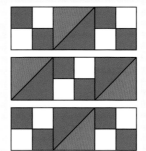

5 Join the rows to complete the block.

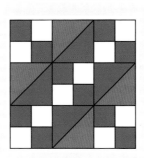

Variations

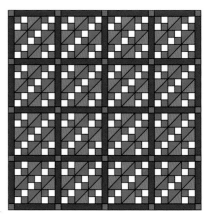

Blocks set with a border and sashings with posts.

When alternate blocks are rotated 90 degrees, a grid of diamonds emerges.

Alternate rows of blocks have been rotated 90 degrees to form a Streak of Lightning pattern.

SKILL LEVEL ▾

TEMPLATES ▾

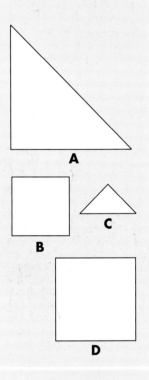

A

B

C

D

FABRICS ▾

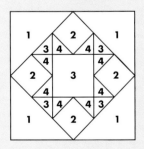

1 *DARK*
2 *MEDIUM LIGHT*
3 *MEDIUM DARK*
4 *LIGHT*

Locked Star

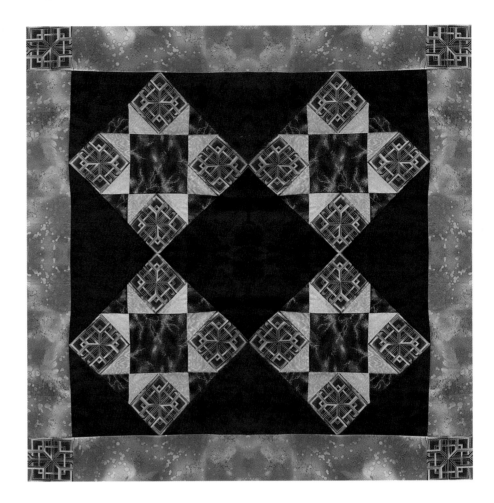

When repeated blocks are joined side by side, the effect is of pieced stars set between plain squares. However, you can vary this effect by using fabrics in different colors on opposite sides of the center square, as shown in the variations opposite. You could also use a feature fabric for the central square. The quilt is finished with a border and corner posts.

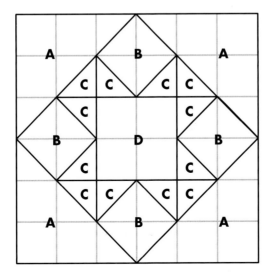

Drafting

Draft the block on a 6 × 6 grid and make the templates.

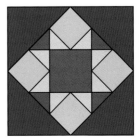

Make a quick sketch of the block and pin scraps of your fabrics to it to use as reference.

Making the block

✂

1 Cut out all the fabric in the required shapes as directed.

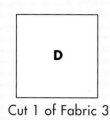

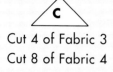

Cut 4 of Fabric 3
Cut 8 of Fabric 4

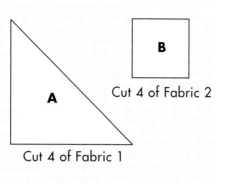

Cut 4 of Fabric 1

Cut 1 of Fabric 3

2 Join pairs of Fabric 4 C patches to each B patch.

 × 4

3 Join pairs of Fabric 3 C patches to two of the pieced units.

 × 2

4 Join the remaining two pieced units to opposite sides of Patch D, then lay out and join the three elements to form the center square.

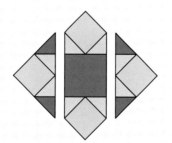

5 Join an A patch to each side of the center square to complete the block.

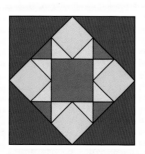

Variations

Blocks set with sashings, border, and posts.

A different fabric has been used for the A patches on opposite sides of the center square.

Memory

TEMPLATES ▾

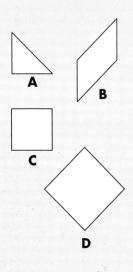

This block, dating from the beginning of the twentieth century, is one of several named Memory. Although some Memory blocks were made from the dresses of a departed loved one, this is such a cheerful pattern that it certainly belies any gloomy associations the name might have. This quilt is finished with a border and corner posts.

FABRICS ▾

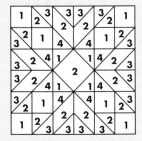

1 DARK
2 MEDIUM DARK
3 LIGHT
4 MEDIUM

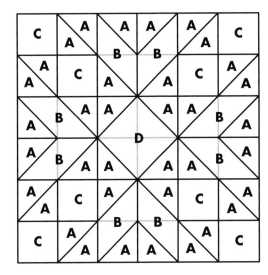

Drafting

Draft the block on a 6 × 6 grid and make the templates.

Make a quick sketch of the block and pin scraps of your fabrics to it to use as reference.

Making the block

✂

1 Cut out all the fabric in the required shapes as directed.

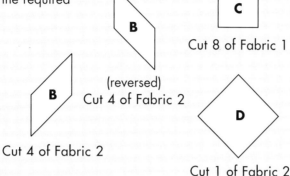

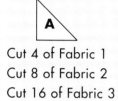

Cut 4 of Fabric 1
Cut 8 of Fabric 2
Cut 16 of Fabric 3
Cut 8 of Fabric 4

Cut 4 of Fabric 2

(reversed)
Cut 4 of Fabric 2

Cut 8 of Fabric 1

Cut 1 of Fabric 2

2 Piece pairs of A patches together, then join these with C patches to form the corner units.

 × 4

3 Piece A, B, and reversed B patches together to form the side units.

 × 4

4 Join the remaining A and D patches to form the center square.

5 Join the pieced units in rows, then join the rows to complete the block.

Variations

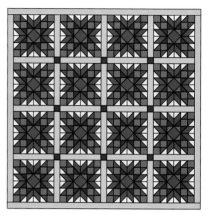

Blocks set with sashings, posts, and a plain border.

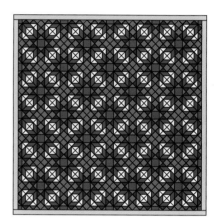

Blocks set on point and finished with a plain border.

When the corner units of each block are rotated 90 degrees, a different pattern emerges.

Roman Pavement

TEMPLATES ▾

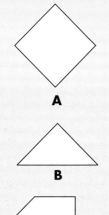

A

B

C

D

FABRICS ▾

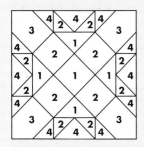

1 *MEDIUM DARK*
2 *DARK*
3 *MEDIUM LIGHT*
4 *LIGHT*

Roman Pavement is an old name for this block, which was published in 1898 as Swing in the Center, a name referring to a square dance call. It is also known as Mrs. Roosevelt's Choice, following a custom popular among quilt makers of naming blocks in honor of particular people. This example is finished with a mitered border.

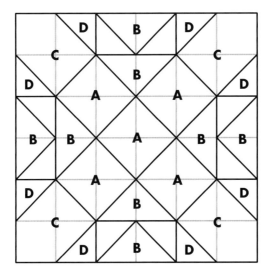

Drafting

Draft the block on a 6 × 6 grid and make the templates.

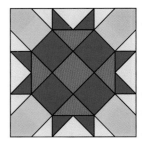

Make a quick sketch of the block and pin scraps of your fabrics to it to use as reference.

Making the block

1 Cut out all the fabric in the required shapes as directed.

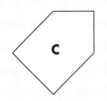

C

Cut 4 of Fabric 3

A

Cut 1 of Fabric 1
Cut 4 of Fabric 2

B

Cut 4 of Fabric 1
Cut 4 of Fabric 4

D

Cut 8 of Fabric 2
Cut 8 of Fabric 4

2 Piece pairs of A and C patches together, then piece the B and D patches together.

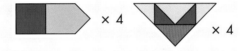

× 4   × 4

3 Join pieced units to form the corner elements.

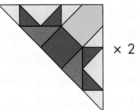

× 2

4 Join the remaining pieced units and A patch to form the diagonal center strip.

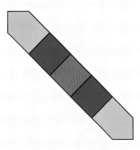

5 Join the three elements to complete the block.

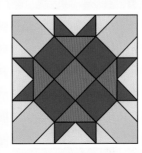

Variations

Blocks set with sashings and a mitered border in the same color.

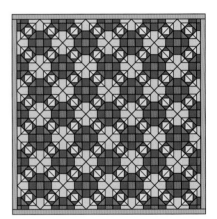

When blocks are set on point, rows of crosses stand out across the surface of the quilt.

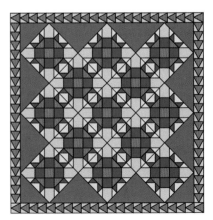

Blocks set on point with plain triangles around the edges. The quilt is finished with a pieced Flying Geese border.

SKILL LEVEL ▾

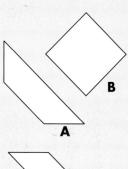

TEMPLATES ▾

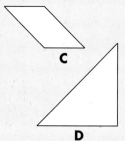

FABRICS ▾

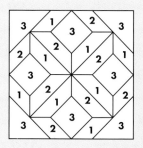

1 DARK
2 MEDIUM
3 LIGHT

Shaded Trail

The four center blades should be pieced in two shades of the same color, so that they appear to be faceted. The third fabric forming the background can be either very light or very dark, depending on the tones you have chosen for the other two fabrics. It is easier to stitch this block by hand using the English patchwork method (see page 30). This example is finished with a border and corner posts.

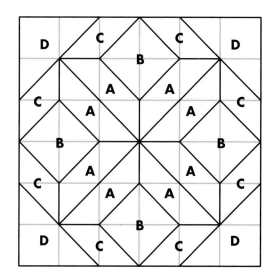

Drafting

Draft the block on a 6 × 6 grid and make the templates.

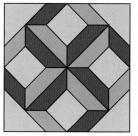

Make a quick sketch of the block and pin scraps of your fabrics to it to use as reference.

Making the block

✂

1 Cut out all the fabric in the required shapes as directed. Cut out the same quantities of paper patches, but without a seam allowance.

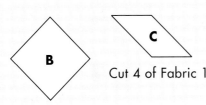

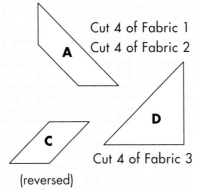

B
Cut 4 of Fabric 3

C
Cut 4 of Fabric 1

A
Cut 4 of Fabric 1
Cut 4 of Fabric 2

D
Cut 4 of Fabric 3

C (reversed)
Cut 4 of Fabric 2

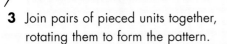

2 Baste or press all the fabric and paper patches together (see pages 30 and 32). Join A, B, C, and reversed C patches together, setting in the corner seams (see page 27).

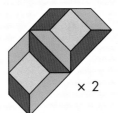

× 4

3 Join pairs of pieced units together, rotating them to form the pattern.

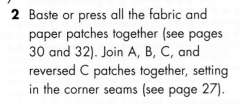

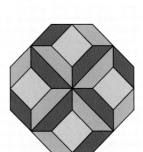

× 2

4 Join the pairs to form the center of the block.

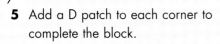

5 Add a D patch to each corner to complete the block.

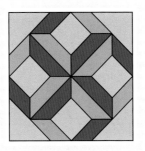

Variations

Blocks set with sashings, posts, and a plain border.

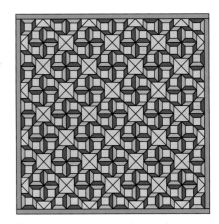

Blocks set on point put the emphasis on the cross in the center of each block.

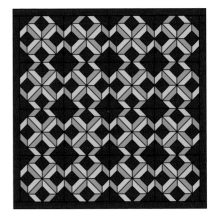

A dark color has been used instead of a light color for the background. A plain border of the same color has been added, providing the minimum of distraction from the cross motifs.

Four Corners

SKILL LEVEL ▾

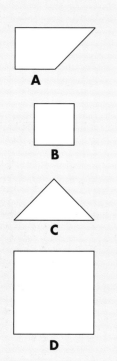

TEMPLATES ▾

A

B

C

D

FABRICS ▾

1 *MEDIUM*
2 *LIGHT*
3 *DARK*
4 *FEATURE*

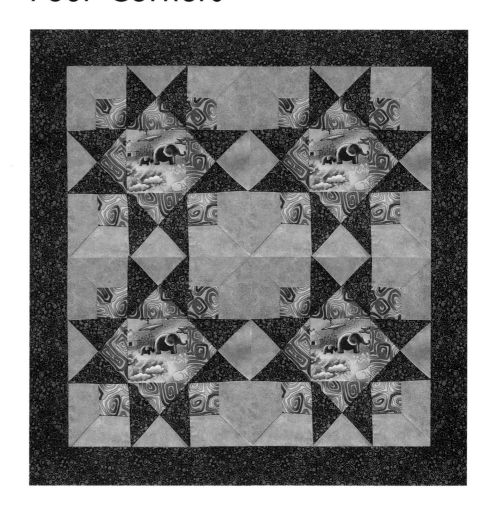

Four Corners is a striking block dating from the 1930s. The large center square is a good opportunity to use a feature fabric, as in this example, or to embellish each block with a quilting design. The mitered border around this quilt echoes the mitered corner units of the blocks.

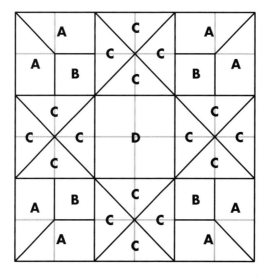

Drafting

Draft the block on a 6 × 6 grid and make the templates.

Make a quick sketch of the block and pin scraps of your fabrics to it to use as reference.

Making the block

1 Cut out all the fabric in the required shapes as directed.

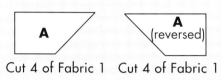

Cut 4 of Fabric 1   Cut 4 of Fabric 1

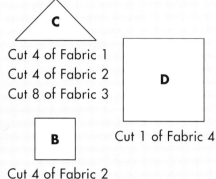

Cut 4 of Fabric 1
Cut 4 of Fabric 2
Cut 8 of Fabric 3

Cut 1 of Fabric 4

Cut 4 of Fabric 2

2 Join an A and reversed A patch to each B patch, setting in the seams at the mitered corners (see page 27).

  × 4

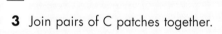

3 Join pairs of C patches together.

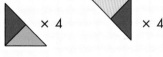 × 4   × 4

4 Join pairs of pieced C patches to form the side units.

 × 4

5 Join the pieced units and D patch in rows, then join the rows to complete the block.

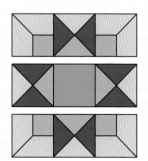

Variations

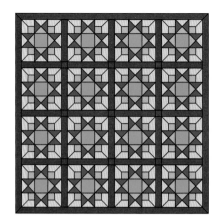

Blocks set with monochrome sashings, posts, and mitered border.

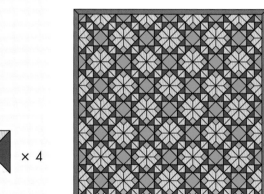

Blocks set on point with half and quarter blocks around the edges and a mitered border.

Blocks set on point with alternate plain squares and triangles. The quilt is finished with a mitered border.

Ocean Waves

TEMPLATES ▾

A

B

Ocean Waves is a popular patchwork theme with many variations, this one dating from 1892. With only two templates needed, the piecing is very easy, but try to cut the triangles for the center strip so that the long sides are on the straight grain of the fabric to avoid distorting the measurements. This is another excellent scrap quilt if the dark/light contrasts are maintained. This quilt is finished with a plain border.

FABRICS ▾

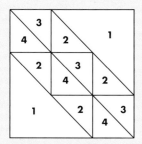

1 DARK
2 MEDIUM LIGHT
3 LIGHT
4 MEDIUM DARK

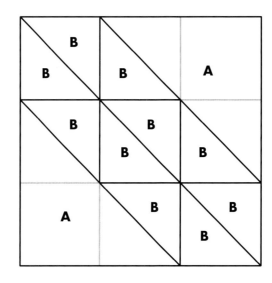

Drafting

Draft the block on a 3 × 3 grid and make the templates.

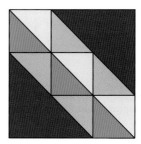

Make a quick sketch of the block and pin scraps of your fabrics to it to use as reference.

Making the block

✄

1 Cut out all the fabric in the required shapes as directed.

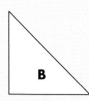

B

Cut 4 of Fabric 2
Cut 3 of Fabric 3
Cut 3 of Fabric 4

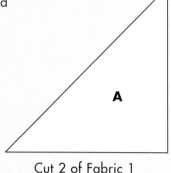

A

Cut 2 of Fabric 1

2 Join pairs of Fabric 3 B and Fabric 4 B patches together.

 × 3

3 Join the remaining B patches to the pieced squares.

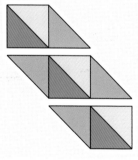

4 Join the pieced units to form the diagonal strip.

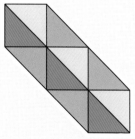

5 Join an A patch to either side of the diagonal strip to complete the block.

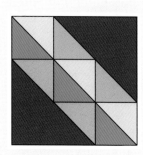

Variations

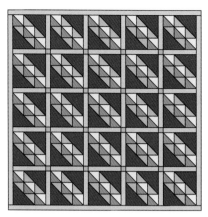

Blocks set with sashings and posts break up the long diagonals of the quilt.

Alternate blocks have been rotated to form a Streak of Lightning pattern.

When alternate rows of the Streak of Lightning formation are rotated, a pattern of squares appears.

SKILL LEVEL ▾

TEMPLATES ▾

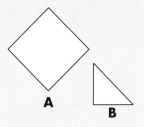

A

B

C

D

FABRICS ▾

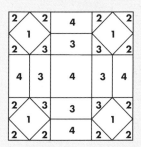

1 *DARK*
2 *LIGHT*
3 *MEDIUM LIGHT*
4 *MEDIUM*

Rolling Stone

Rolling Stone is also known as Wedding Ring, a name that reflects the visual impression created by the block. Its romantic associations would certainly make it an ideal block for a wedding quilt. Here, it is finished with a mitered border.

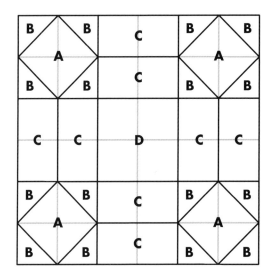

Drafting

Draft the block on a 6 × 6 grid and make the templates.

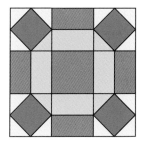

Make a quick sketch of the block and pin scraps of your fabrics to it to use as reference.

Making the block

1 Cut out all the fabric in the required shapes as directed.

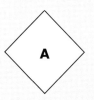

Cut 4 of Fabric 1

Cut 12 of Fabric 2
Cut 4 of Fabric 3

C

Cut 4 of Fabric 3
Cut 4 of Fabric 4

D

Cut 1 of Fabric 4

2 Join a B patch to each side of the A patches to form the corner units.

 × 4

3 Join pairs of C patches together.

 × 4

4 Join the pieced units and D patch in rows, rotating them to form the pattern.

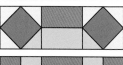

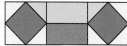

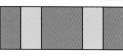

5 Join the rows to complete the block.

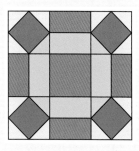

Variations

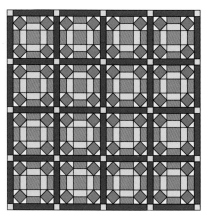

Blocks set with a border and sashings interspersed with posts in the same color as the ring design of the block.

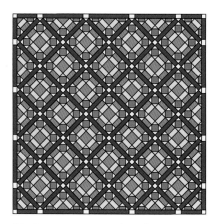

Blocks set on point with sashings, border, and posts.

The innermost triangles in the corner units of each block have been cut in Fabric 1 instead of Fabric 3. This eliminates the ring design and creates a strong pattern of crosses. The blocks are set on point and finished with a plain border.

Basket of Scraps

TEMPLATES ▾

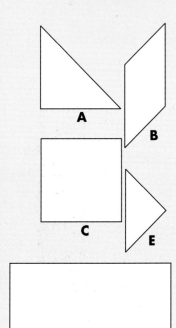

A

B

C

E

D

FABRICS ▾

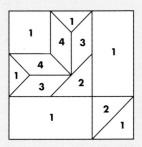

1 LIGHT
2 MEDIUM DARK
3 DARK
4 MEDIUM LIGHT

This simple nine-patch block can produce some stunning quilts. As the name suggests, the block really invites you to make it from scraps, but it also works well if you use the same fabrics in every block. The only difficult thing is that patches must be set into the petal shapes, but you could use the English patchwork method to avoid this if you prefer (see page 30). This quilt is finished with a mitered border.

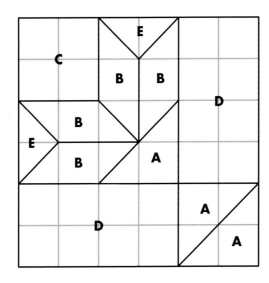

Drafting

Draft the block on a 6 × 6 grid and make the templates.

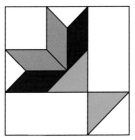

Make a quick sketch of the block and pin scraps of your fabrics to it to use as reference.

Making the block

✄

1 Cut out all the fabric in the required shapes as directed.

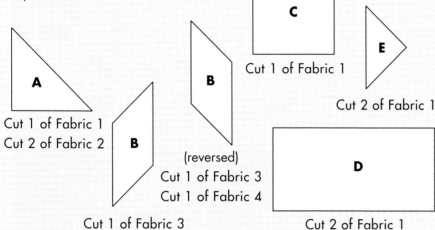

A
Cut 1 of Fabric 1
Cut 2 of Fabric 2

B
Cut 1 of Fabric 3
Cut 1 of Fabric 4

B (reversed)
Cut 1 of Fabric 3
Cut 1 of Fabric 4

C
Cut 1 of Fabric 1

E
Cut 2 of Fabric 1

D
Cut 2 of Fabric 1

2 Piece the B and reversed B patches together to form petals, then add a Fabric 2 A patch to one corner.

3 Add the C and E patches to complete the corner unit, setting in the seams (see page 27).

4 Join the remaining two A patches together, then add a D patch.

5 Join the remaining D patch to one side of the corner unit, then join the two pieced elements to complete the block.

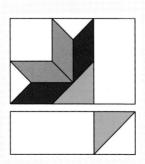

Variations

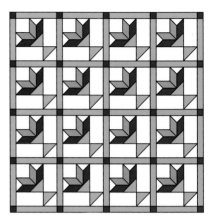

Blocks set with sashings, border, and posts.

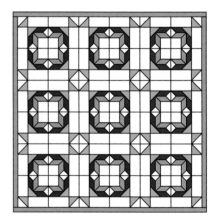

Blocks have been rotated so that the petal shapes meet at the center of each group of four blocks to form a different pattern.

The same rotated pattern is used here, but this time the light background in the blocks has been replaced with dark fabric. The rotated blocks have also been set with sashings and posts.

SKILL LEVEL ▾

TEMPLATES ▾

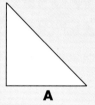

A

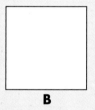

B

FABRICS ▾

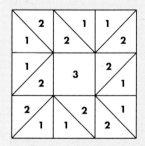

1 *MEDIUM LIGHT*
2 *MEDIUM DARK*
3 *FEATURE*

Box Quilt

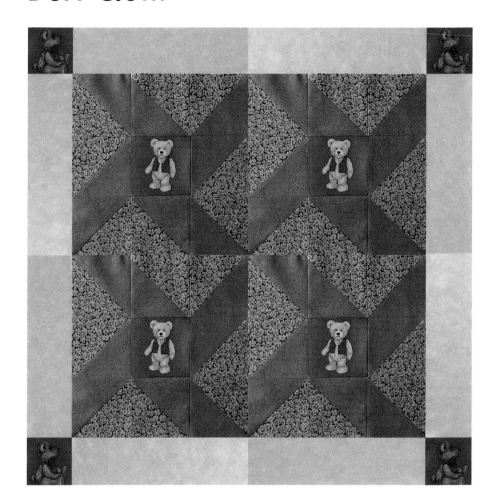

Repeated Box Quilt blocks do indeed suggest box shapes, with the angles producing an interesting swirling effect. At the same time, a pattern of pinwheels emerges. This is an ideal block for beginners because the piecing is very easy. This quilt has a border with corner posts and uses a feature fabric for the center square, although you could replace this with a light fabric if you prefer.

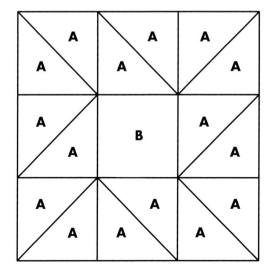

Drafting

Draft the block on a 3 × 3 grid and make the templates.

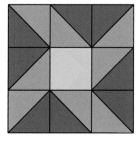

Make a quick sketch of the block and pin scraps of your fabrics to it to use as reference.

Making the block

1 Cut out all the fabric in the required shapes as directed.

Cut 8 of Fabric 1   Cut 1 of Fabric 3
Cut 8 of Fabric 2

2 Join pairs of B patches together. If you are making a lot of blocks, use the chain piecing method (see page 28).

 × 8

3 Lay out and join the pieced units and B patch in rows, rotating them to form the pattern.

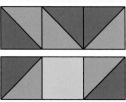

4 Join the rows to complete the block.

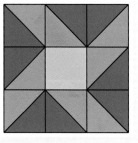

Variations

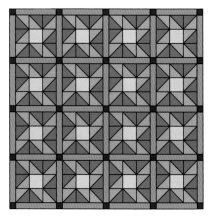

Blocks set with sashings, border, and posts.

Blocks set on point with half and quarter blocks around the edges and a plain border.

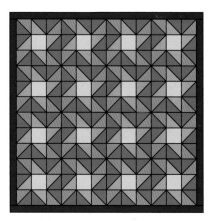

Four of the outer triangles of each block are cut in a different color fabric. This small change to the coloring results in a distinctive pattern of stars set within pinwheels.

Claws Variation

TEMPLATES ▾

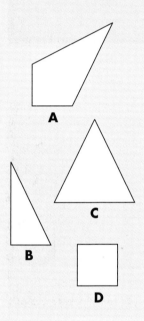

A

B

C

D

This is a slight variation of a modern block that, when repeated, produces the effect of a Kaleidoscope block set with pieced sashings. This example is finished with a border and corner posts. Many nine-patch blocks lend themselves to interesting variations by rotating some of the units from which they are made. A good example of this is shown opposite.

FABRICS ▾

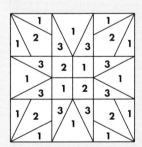

1 *MEDIUM*
2 *DARK*
3 *LIGHT*

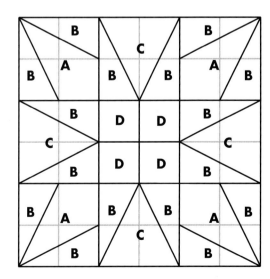

Drafting

Draft the block on a 6 × 6 grid and make the templates.

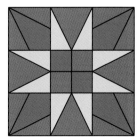

Make a quick sketch of the block and pin scraps of your fabrics to it to use as reference.

Making the block

1 Cut out all the fabric in the required shapes as directed.

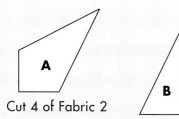

A
Cut 4 of Fabric 2

B
Cut 4 of Fabric 1
Cut 4 of Fabric 3

B (reversed)
Cut 4 of Fabric 1
Cut 4 of Fabric 3

C
Cut 4 of Fabric 1

D
Cut 2 of Fabric 1
Cut 2 of Fabric 2

2 Join a Fabric 1 B and reversed B patch to each A patch to form the corner units.

 × 4

3 Join a Fabric 3 B and reversed B patch to each C patch to form the side units.

 × 4

4 Piece the D patches together to form the center square.

5 Join the units in rows, rotating them to form the pattern, then join the rows to complete the block.

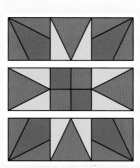

Variations

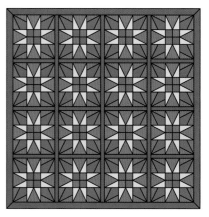

Blocks set with narrow sashings and a wider mitered border.

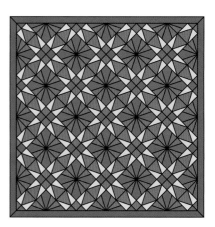

Blocks set on point with half and quarter blocks around the edges and a mitered border.

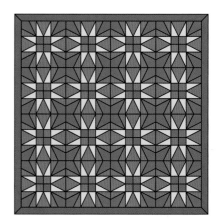

When the four corner units in each block are rotated 180 degrees, a different pattern appears. The effect is of another block called World Without End.

TEMPLATES ▾

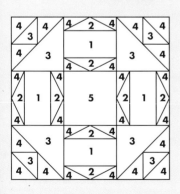

A
B
C
D E
F

FABRICS ▾

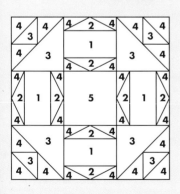

1 MEDIUM
2 MEDIUM LIGHT
3 DARK
4 LIGHT
5 MEDIUM DARK

Joseph's Coat

According to one account, Joseph's Coat, being composed of many patches, was especially designed to make use of the last remnants of the scrap bag. Indeed, in Pennsylvania it was known as Scrap Bag. However, whether you stick to five fabrics, as shown here, or use different fabrics for each block, it creates a superb quilt. This example is finished with a border and corner posts.

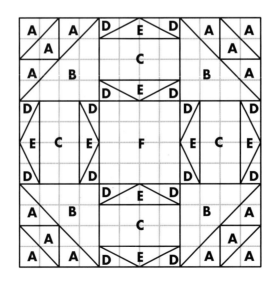

Drafting

Draft the block on a 12 × 12 grid and make the templates.

Make a quick sketch of the block and pin scraps of your fabrics to it to use as reference.

Making the block

✂

1 Cut out all the fabric in the required shapes as directed.

C
Cut 4 of Fabric 1

E
Cut 8 of Fabric 2

D
Cut 8 of Fabric 4

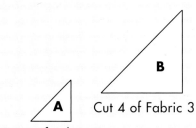
B
Cut 4 of Fabric 3

A
Cut 4 of Fabric 3
Cut 12 of Fabric 4

D
(reversed)
Cut 8 of Fabric 4

F
Cut 1 of Fabric 5

2 Piece a D and reversed D patch to each E patch.

 × 8

3 Join two pieced units to each C patch to form the side elements.

 × 4

4 Piece four A patches together, then add a B patch to form the corner units.

 × 4

🪡

5 Join the pieced units and F patch in rows, then join the rows to complete the block.

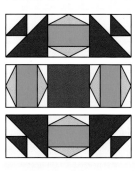

Variations

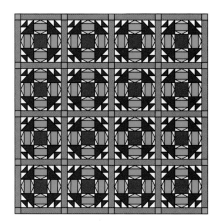

Blocks set with sashings, border, and posts.

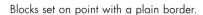

Blocks set on point with a plain border.

Arrows

TEMPLATES ▾

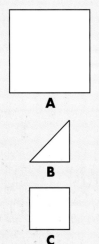

A

B

C

Because this block has only diagonal symmetry, it lends itself to some interesting variations and settings. Only three templates and three fabrics are needed, so this is not a difficult block to make. This example is finished with a mitered border and uses a feature fabric for two of the A patches, but you could replace this with any medium-colored fabric if you prefer.

FABRICS ▾

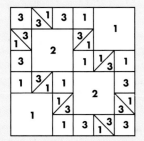

1 *LIGHT*
2 *FEATURE*
3 *DARK*

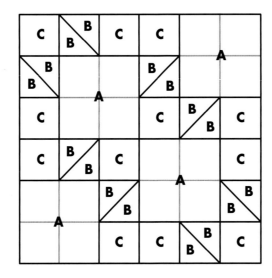

Drafting

Draft the block on a 6 × 6 grid and make the templates.

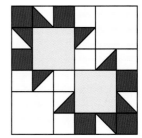

Make a quick sketch of the block and pin scraps of your fabrics to it to use as reference.

Making the block

1 Cut out all the fabric in the required shapes as directed.

 A

Cut 2 of Fabric 1
Cut 2 of Fabric 2

B

Cut 8 of Fabric 1
Cut 8 of Fabric 3

 C

Cut 6 of Fabric 1
Cut 6 of Fabric 3

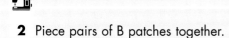

2 Piece pairs of B patches together.

 × 8

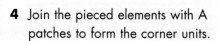

3 Join the pieced units with C patches.

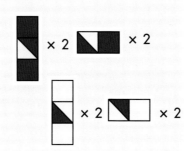

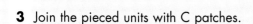

4 Join the pieced elements with A patches to form the corner units.

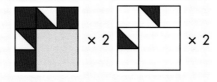

5 Join the units in rows, rotating them to form the pattern, then join the rows to complete the block.

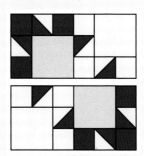

Variations

Blocks set on point with a plain border.

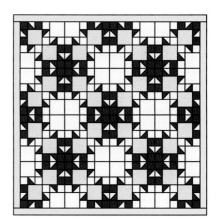

Alternate blocks have been rotated 90 degrees to create a pattern of stars surrounded by a circle of squares.

A different color has been used for the Fabric 1 A patches.

Wyoming Valley

SKILL LEVEL ▾

TEMPLATES ▾

FABRICS ▾

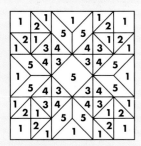

1 *DARK*
2 *MEDIUM LIGHT*
3 *MEDIUM*
4 *LIGHT*
5 *MEDIUM DARK*

This delightful nine-patch star, credited to Nancy Cabot, was published in the 1930s in a syndicated column in the *Chicago Tribune*. Hundreds of Cabot's patterns were sold by mail order. Here, it is finished with a border and corner posts. When blocks of Wyoming Valley are repeated, a complex pattern of stars is revealed across the quilt's surface.

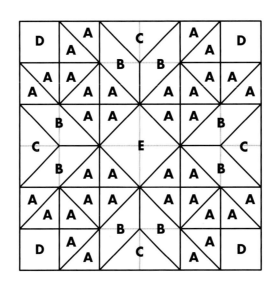

Drafting

Draft the block on a 6 × 6 grid and make the templates.

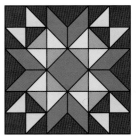

Make a quick sketch of the block and pin scraps of your fabrics to it to use as reference.

Making the block

1 Cut out all the fabric in the required shapes as directed.

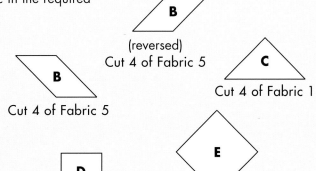

A

Cut 12 of Fabric 1
Cut 8 of Fabric 2
Cut 8 of Fabric 3
Cut 8 of Fabric 4

B

Cut 4 of Fabric 5

B (reversed)
Cut 4 of Fabric 5

C
Cut 4 of Fabric 1

D
Cut 4 of Fabric 1

E
Cut 1 of Fabric 5

2 Join pairs of A patches together, then piece these with D patches to form the corner units.

 × 4

3 Piece two A, one B, one reversed B, and one C patch together to form the side units, setting in the seams where the C patch is added (see page 27).

 × 4

4 Join the remaining A patches to each side of Patch E to form the center square.

5 Join the pieced units in rows, rotating them to form the pattern, then join the rows to complete the block.

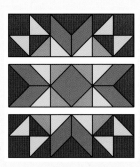

Variations

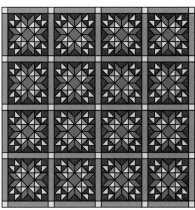

Blocks set with sashings, border, and posts.

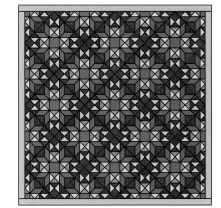

Blocks set on point with half and quarter blocks around the edges and a plain border.

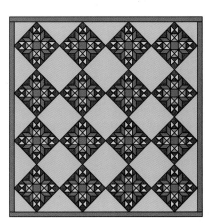

Blocks set on point with alternate plain squares and triangles. The quilt is framed with a plain border.

SKILL LEVEL ▾

TEMPLATES ▾

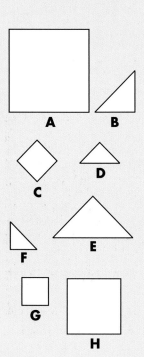

A B C D E F G H

FABRICS ▾

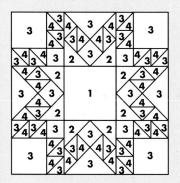

1 FEATURE
2 DARK
3 LIGHT
4 MEDIUM

Star Diamond

This nine-patch star is one of the more complex blocks that are often known as feathered stars. Although it looks complicated, the piecing is broken down into manageable units. Take great care when piecing the corner and side units, however, because the small triangular and square patches are very similar in size and are cut in the same fabrics. This example is finished with a border and corner posts.

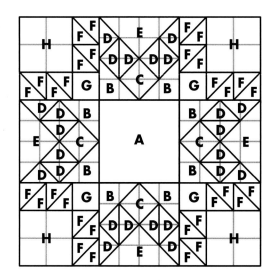

Drafting

Draft a 3 × 3 grid, then divide the corner units into 3 × 3 and the side units into 4 × 4. Make templates.

Make a quick sketch of the block and pin scraps of your fabrics to it to use as reference.

Making the block

✄

1 Cut out all the fabric in the required shapes as directed.

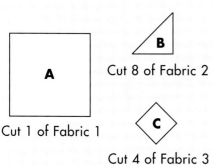

A

Cut 1 of Fabric 1

B

Cut 8 of Fabric 2

C

Cut 4 of Fabric 3

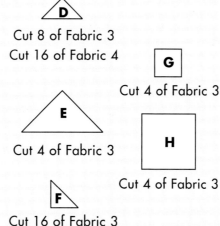

D

Cut 8 of Fabric 3
Cut 16 of Fabric 4

E

Cut 4 of Fabric 3

F

Cut 16 of Fabric 3
Cut 16 of Fabric 4

G

Cut 4 of Fabric 3

H

Cut 4 of Fabric 3

2 Join pairs of F patches together, then piece them with G and H patches to form the corner units.

 × 4

3 Join eight pairs of D patches together, then piece them with C and E patches and the remaining D patches.

× 4

4 Add B patches to complete the side units.

 × 4

5 Join the pieced units and Patch A in rows, then join the rows to complete the block.

Variations

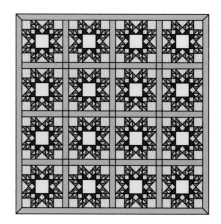

Blocks set with sashings, posts, and a mitered border.

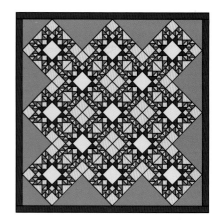

Blocks set on point with plain triangles around the edges and a plain border.

Five blocks set on point with plain triangles around the edges. The quilt is finished with a narrow border and then a wider pieced border, making this a striking design for a wall quilt.

Illinois

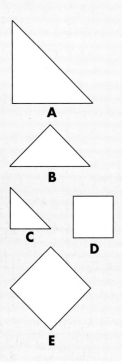

A

B

C

D

E

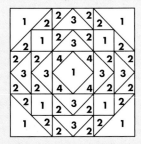

1 *MEDIUM LIGHT*
2 *LIGHT*
3 *DARK*
4 *MEDIUM*

This Illinois block quilt is finished with a border and corner posts. However, if you are making lots of blocks, you could sew the side units using the chain piecing method (see page 28) and then use any leftover units to make a pieced border, as shown in the variations opposite. Alternatively, save them for another quilting project.

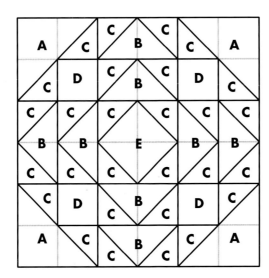

Drafting

Draft the block on a 6 × 6 grid and make the templates.

Make a quick sketch of the block and pin scraps of your fabrics to it to use as reference.

Making the block

>✂

1 Cut out all the fabric in the required shapes as directed.

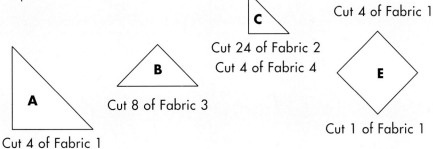

A
Cut 4 of Fabric 1

B
Cut 8 of Fabric 3

C
Cut 24 of Fabric 2
Cut 4 of Fabric 4

D
Cut 4 of Fabric 1

E
Cut 1 of Fabric 1

2 Join two Fabric 2 C patches to each D patch, then add an A patch to complete the corner units.

 × 4

3 Join two Fabric 2 C patches to each B patch, then sew pairs of pieced elements together to complete the side units.

 × 4

4 Piece the center square by sewing a Fabric 4 C patch to each side of Patch E.

5 Join the pieced units in rows, rotating them to form the pattern, then join the rows to complete the block.

Variations

A plain border separates the center field of the quilt from the Sawtooth border around the outer edge. This was pieced from units left over from using the chain piecing method to make the elements of the block.

Blocks set on point with plain triangles around the edges and a plain border.

A monochromatic version of the Illinois block.

SKILL LEVEL ▾

TEMPLATES ▾

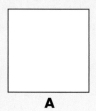

A

B

C   **D**

FABRICS ▾

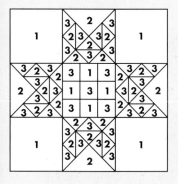

1 *MEDIUM*
2 *MEDIUM DARK*
3 *DARK*

Dolley Madison's Star

As wife of the fourth president of the United States, Dolley Madison was "Mistress of the White House" for 16 years. She became known for her beauty and prowess as a hostess and for having a social conscience. The block is of Virginian origin, dating from the early nineteenth century, when it would have been pieced in red, white, and blue to signify the new republic. Here, it is finished with a border with corner posts.

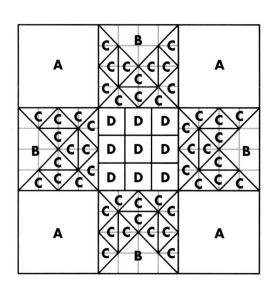

Drafting

Draft a 3 × 3 grid, then divide the center unit into 3 × 3 and the side units into 4 × 4. Make templates.

Make a quick sketch of the block and pin scraps of your fabrics to it to use as reference.

Making the block

✂

1 Cut out all the fabric in the required shapes as directed.

Cut 4 of Fabric 1

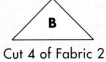

Cut 4 of Fabric 2

Cut 20 of Fabric 2
Cut 28 of Fabric 3

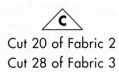

Cut 4 of Fabric 1
Cut 5 of Fabric 3

2 Join groups of four C patches together.

 × 4    × 8

3 Join pairs of pieced units and B patches together, then join these pairs along the diagonal seam to complete the side units.

 × 4

4 Piece the center square from D patches.

5 Join the pieced units and A patches in rows, then join the rows to complete the block.

Variations

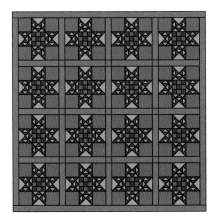

Blocks set with sashings, posts, and a plain border.

Here, the dark fabric has been replaced with a light fabric, which has also been used for the sashings and border. The blocks are set on point with half and quarter blocks around the edges.

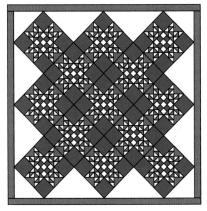

Blocks pieced in traditional red, white, and blue and set on point with plain white triangles around the edges and a plain red border.

SKILL LEVEL ▾

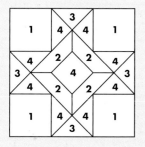

TEMPLATES ▾

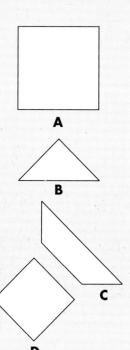

A

B

C

D

FABRICS ▾

1 MEDIUM DARK
2 MEDIUM LIGHT
3 LIGHT
4 DARK

Braced Star

Braced Star is based on a traditional Ohio Star block with a pieced square set on point inside it. The corners of the center square are mitered, so a little care is needed when piecing it. The rest, though, is not difficult. This example is finished with a mitered border. When blocks are repeated, the corner units meet to form large squares, so if you use plain fabric for these, you can embellish them with a quilting pattern.

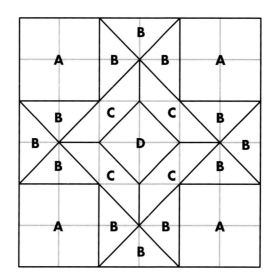

Drafting

Draft the block on a 6 × 6 grid and make the templates.

Make a quick sketch of the block and pin scraps of your fabrics to it to use as reference.

Making the block

1 Cut out all the fabric in the required shapes as directed.

A

Cut 4 of Fabric 1

B

Cut 4 of Fabric 3
Cut 8 of Fabric 4

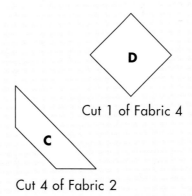

C

Cut 4 of Fabric 2

D

Cut 1 of Fabric 4

2 Join two C patches to opposite sides of Patch D.

3 Join the remaining C patches to the other two sides of Patch D, setting in the seams (see page 27).

4 Join pairs of Fabric 4 B patches to each A patch, then add pairs of Fabric 3 B patches to two of these pieced units.

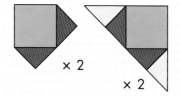

× 2

× 2

5 Join the pieced units to form the diagonal center strip, then join all the units to complete the block.

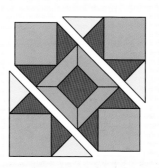

Variations

Blocks set with monochrome sashings, posts, and plain border.

Blocks set on point with plain light-colored triangles around the edges and a plain dark border.

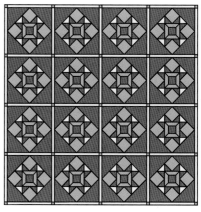

Blocks set on point with a plain triangle added to each side and narrow sashings, border, and posts.

SKILL LEVEL ▾

TEMPLATES ▾

A

B

FABRICS ▾

3 2	4	2 3
4	1	4
3 2	4	2 3

1 MEDIUM DARK
2 LIGHT
3 DARK
4 MEDIUM

Calico Puzzle

Here is a really easy block that has hidden appeal—repeated blocks reveal a pattern of pinwheels joined with sashings and posts, making it look a lot more complicated than it really is. It makes a wonderful scrap quilt if you emphasize the light/dark contrast in the pinwheels. This block, finished here with a plain border, is a gift to beginners or to anyone who wants to make a quick quilt.

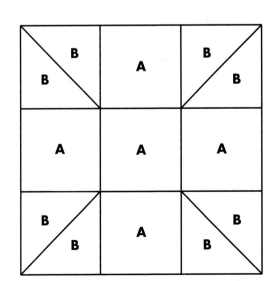

Drafting

Draft the block on a 3 × 3 grid and make the templates.

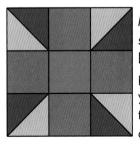

Make a quick sketch of the block and pin scraps of your fabrics to it to use as reference.

Making the block

1 Cut out all the fabric in the required shapes as directed.

Cut 1 of Fabric 1   Cut 4 of Fabric 2
Cut 4 of Fabric 4   Cut 4 of Fabric 3

2 Piece pairs of B patches together.

 × 4

3 Join two pieced units to opposite sides of a Fabric 4 A patch to form the top and bottom row.

 × 2

4 Join the remaining A patches together to form the center row.

5 Join the rows to complete the block.

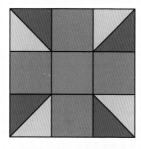

Variations

Blocks set on point with a narrow border and corner posts in the same colors as the central cross of the block.

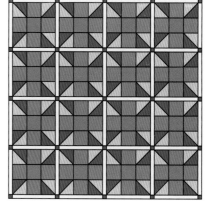

Make Calico Puzzle look even more impressive by setting the blocks with narrow sashings, border, and posts.

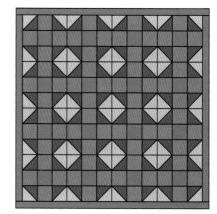

Rotate each corner unit so that the dark patches are at the center of the block to form a completely different pattern.

SKILL LEVEL ▾

TEMPLATES ▾

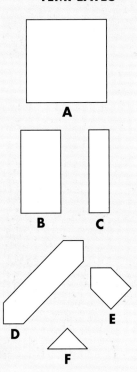

A

B   C

D

E

F

Garden Maze

Garden Maze, finished here with a mitered border, is an intriguing block that, when repeated, produces a complex interlaced pattern that forces the viewer to look closely to see where blocks begin and end. It requires careful piecing to get the pattern right, but this is a good block to choose if you want to create a big impression. Make sure you choose fabrics with good dark/light contrast.

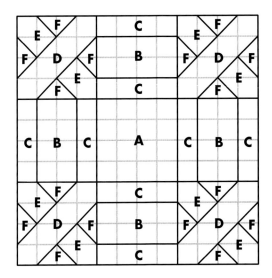

Drafting

Draft the block on a 12 × 12 grid and make the templates.

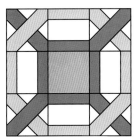

Make a quick sketch of the block and pin scraps of your fabrics to it to use as reference.

FABRICS ▾

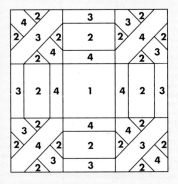

1 *MEDIUM DARK*
2 *LIGHT*
3 *MEDIUM LIGHT*
4 *DARK*

Making the block

>✂

1 Cut out all the fabric in the required shapes as directed.

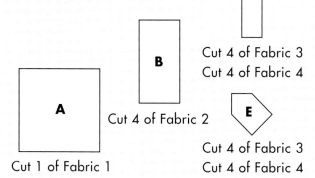

Cut 1 of Fabric 1

Cut 4 of Fabric 2

Cut 4 of Fabric 3
Cut 4 of Fabric 4

Cut 2 of Fabric 3
Cut 2 of Fabric 4

Cut 4 of Fabric 3
Cut 4 of Fabric 4

Cut 16 of Fabric 2

2 Piece two F patches to each E patch.

 × 4   × 4

3 Join the pieced elements with D patches to form the corner units.

 × 2   × 2

4 Join pairs of C patches to each B patch to form the side units.

 × 4

5 Join the pieced units and Patch A in rows, noting the placement of the corner units carefully, then join the rows to complete the block.

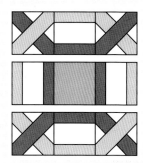

Variations

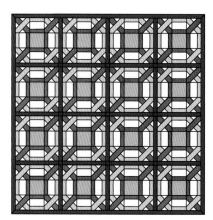

When blocks are set with narrow sashings, an even more complex effect is achieved, with the interlacing pattern appearing to lie beneath another layer.

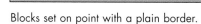

Blocks set on point with a plain border.

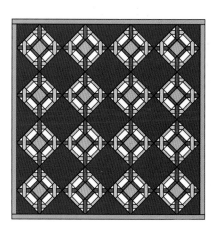

Blocks set on point with alternate plain squares and triangles.

Compass Kaleidoscope

SKILL LEVEL ▾

TEMPLATES ▾

A

B

C

D

FABRICS ▾

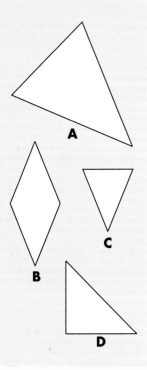

1 *LIGHT*
2 *DARK*
3 *MEDIUM*

Compass Kaleidoscope is a variation on a traditional Kaleidoscope pattern, with repeated blocks forming an interesting design of circles over the quilt surface. This is a lovely pattern for a scrap quilt, and will still create the effect of circles as long as you maintain the light/dark contrast in each block. This example is finished with a mitered border.

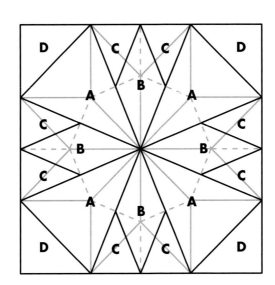

Drafting

Draft the block on an 8-pointed star grid and make the templates.

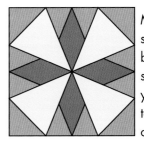

Make a quick sketch of the block and pin scraps of your fabrics to it to use as reference.

Making the block

✂

1 Cut out all the fabric in the required shapes as directed.

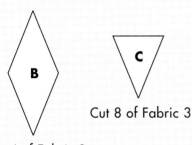

B
Cut 4 of Fabric 2

C
Cut 8 of Fabric 3

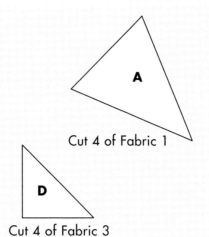

A
Cut 4 of Fabric 1

D
Cut 4 of Fabric 3

2 Join pairs of C patches to each B patch.

 × 4

3 Join the pieced units with pairs of A patches.

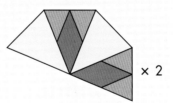 × 2

4 Join the two elements to form the center of the block.

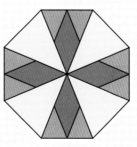

5 Add a D patch at each corner to complete the block.

Variations

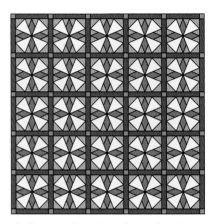

Blocks set with wide sashings, border, and posts.

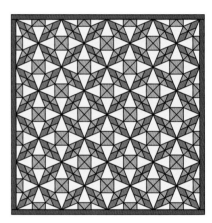

Blocks set on point with quarter and half blocks around the edges and a plain border.

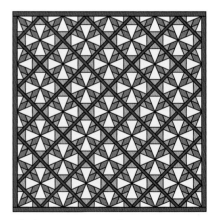

Blocks set on point with narrow sashings and a plain border.

Star of the East

SKILL LEVEL ▾

TEMPLATES ▾

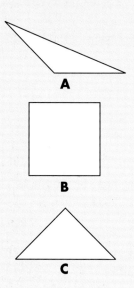

A

B

C

FABRICS ▾

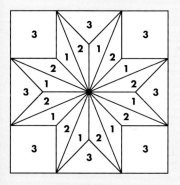

1 *MEDIUM*
2 *LIGHT*
3 *DARK*

Star of the East is a delightful eight-pointed star in which the faceted rays cause it to stand out from its background in a striking way. An alternative to setting in the patches around the star is to appliqué the star onto a square of background fabric. This quilt is finished with a mitered border.

Drafting

Draft the block on an 8-pointed star grid and make the templates.

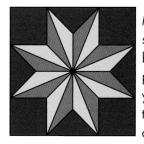

Make a quick sketch of the block and pin scraps of your fabrics to it to use as reference.

Making the block

1 Cut out all the fabric in the required shapes as directed.

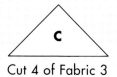
Cut 4 of Fabric 3

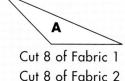
Cut 8 of Fabric 1
Cut 8 of Fabric 2

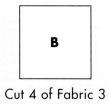
Cut 4 of Fabric 3

2 Join pairs of A patches together.

 × 8

3 Join four pieced units to make each half of the star.

 × 2

4 Join the two halves together.

5 Add the B and C patches around the star to complete the block, setting in the seams (see page 27).

Variations

Blocks set with sashings and a plain border.

Blocks set on point with a plain border.

Blocks set on point with a plain border and narrow sashings and posts.

SKILL LEVEL ▾

TEMPLATES ▾

A

B

C

FABRICS ▾

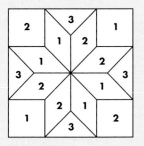

1 *MEDIUM*
2 *LIGHT*
3 *DARK*

Sunshine and Shadow

Sunshine and Shadow is a relatively modern block, first published in 1942, that produces some interesting secondary patterns when blocks are repeated. This example is finished with a border and corner posts.

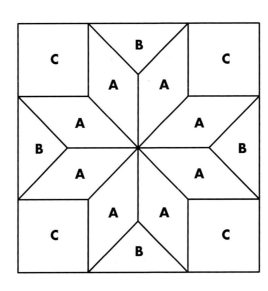

Drafting

Draft the block on an 8-pointed star grid and make the templates.

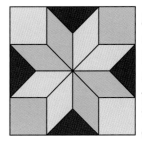

Make a quick sketch of the block and pin scraps of your fabrics to it to use as reference.

Making the block

1 Cut out all the fabric in the required shapes as directed.

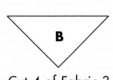

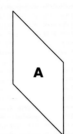

B
Cut 4 of Fabric 3

C
Cut 2 of Fabric 1
Cut 2 of Fabric 2

A
Cut 4 of Fabric 1
Cut 4 of Fabric 2

2 Piece A patches together to make each half of the star.

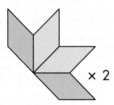

× 2

3 Join the two halves of the star.

4 Add the B patches, setting in the seams (see page 27).

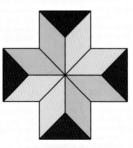

5 Add the C patches, again setting in the seams, to complete the block.

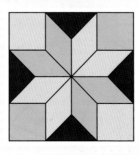

Variations

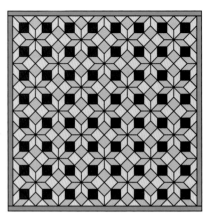

Blocks set on point with quarter and half blocks around the edges and a plain border.

Blocks set on point with sashings, posts, and a plain border.

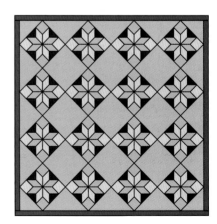

Blocks set on point with alternate plain squares and triangles.

Basic Log Cabin

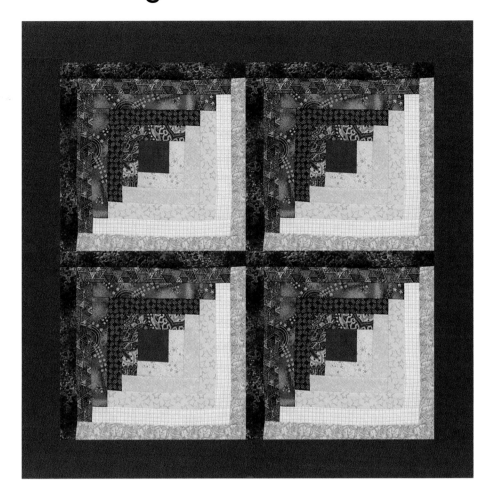

The Basic Log Cabin quilt, one of the most popular patchwork patterns ever, can be made from scrap or repeated fabrics. Many different patterns can be produced by changing the arrangement of the blocks in the quilt. You do not need templates for this block and can piece it as described here or use the foundation piecing technique (see page 31). This example is finished with a plain border.

SKILL LEVEL ▾

MEASUREMENTS ▾

These measurements, which include seam allowances, will make a 12-inch (30-cm) block.

A
2½ × 2½ inches
(6.2 × 6.2 cm)

B
1½ inches
(3.7 cm) wide

FABRICS ▾

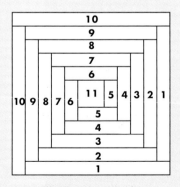

1–5 *LIGHT*
6–10 *DARK*
11 *MEDIUM*

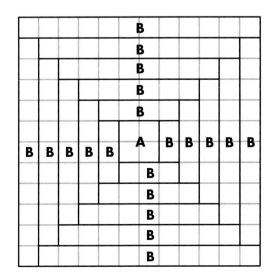

Drafting

Draft the block on a 12 × 12 grid. Measure the square and strip width, and add seam allowances.

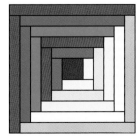

Make a quick sketch of the block and pin scraps of your fabrics to it to use as reference.

Making the block

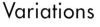

1 Cut out the center square and long strips of fabric (these will be cut to length as you work around the block). Keep cutting batches of fabric as you need it if you are making several blocks.

A

Cut 1 of Fabric 11

B

Cut 1 each of Fabrics 1–10

2 Sew a Fabric 5 light strip to one side of the center square, cutting it to the required length. Sew another Fabric 5 strip to the adjacent side of the square, overlapping it as shown.

3 Sew Fabric 6 dark strips to the opposite two sides, cutting them to the required length and overlapping them as before.

4 Add Fabric 4 light strips and then Fabric 7 dark strips to form the second round.

5 Repeat for each round of the square until you have added five strips to each side, keeping the light and dark fabrics on opposite sides of the block.

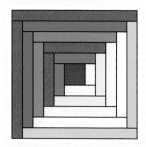

Variations

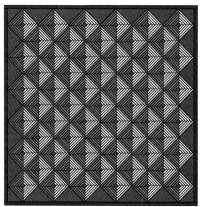

Blocks set on point with plain triangles around the edges in the same color as the center squares.

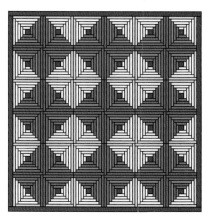

Blocks have been rotated so that the dark areas meet at the center of each group of four blocks to form a pattern known as Light and Dark.

Here, the rotation of the blocks forms concentric light and dark diamonds, known as the Barn Raising pattern.

Chevron Log Cabin

SKILL LEVEL ▾

MEASUREMENTS ▾

These measurements, which include seam allowances, will make a 12-inch (30.3-cm) block.

A
3½ × 3½ inch
(8.7 × 8.7 cm)

B
2 inches (5 cm) wide

FABRICS ▾

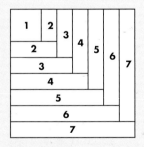

1,3,5,7 *DARK*
2,4,6 *LIGHT*

In this easy variation on the Basic Log Cabin block, alternating strips of light and dark fabrics create a chevron effect that, in turn, produces some interesting variations when several blocks are arranged in a quilt. Again, it is not necessary to make templates; just cut strips of the required width, then cut each one to the right length when it has been sewn around the corner square. This example is finished with a mitered border.

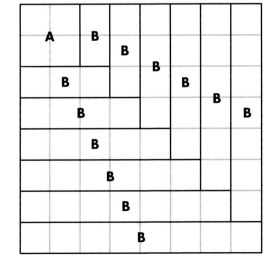

Drafting

Draft the block on an 8 × 8 grid. Measure the square and strip width, and add seam allowances.

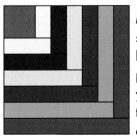

Make a quick sketch of the block and pin scraps of your fabrics to it to use as reference.

Making the block

1 Cut out the corner square and long strips of fabric (these will be cut to length as you work around the block). Keep cutting batches of fabric as you need it if you are making several blocks.

Cut 1 of Fabric 1

Cut 1 each of Fabrics 2–7

2 Sew a Fabric 2 light strip to one side of the corner square, cutting it to the required length. Sew another Fabric 2 strip to the adjacent side of the square, overlapping it as shown.

3 Add Fabric 3 dark strips to the two light strips, cutting them to the required length and overlapping them as before.

4 Repeat this process with Fabric 4 light strips.

5 Continue alternating dark and light strips to complete the block.

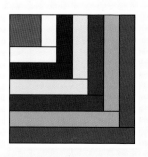

Variations

Blocks set on point with half and quarter blocks around the edges.

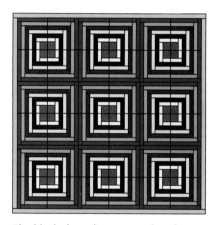

The blocks have been rotated so that the dark corner squares meet at the center of each group of four blocks to form a pattern of large squares.

Rotating the blocks in a different arrangement produces this visually complex pattern of interlocking squares.

Courthouse Steps

MEASUREMENTS ▾

These measurements, which include seam allowances, will make a 12-inch (30-cm) block.

A

2½ × 2½ inches
(6.2 × 6.2 cm)

B

1½ inches
(3.7 cm) wide

FABRICS ▾

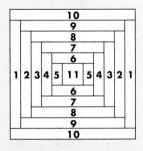

1–5 LIGHT
6–10 DARK
11 MEDIUM

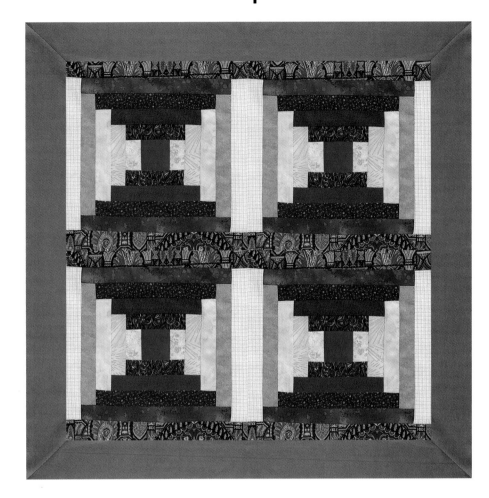

In this variation on the Basic Log Cabin block, finished here with a mitered border, the dark and light fabrics are placed opposite each other, rather than on two adjacent sides. Although you could make templates and cut the "logs" to the exact sizes required, it is easier to cut long strips of fabric and trim them to the required length after you have sewn them in place.

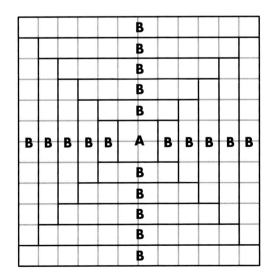

Drafting

Draft the block on a 12 × 12 grid. Measure the square and strip width, and add seam allowances.

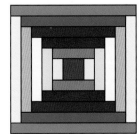

Make a quick sketch of the block and pin scraps of your fabrics to it to use as reference.

Making the block

1 Cut out the center square and long strips of fabric (these will be cut to length as you work around the block). Keep cutting batches of fabric as you need it if you are making several blocks.

2 Sew a Fabric 5 light strip to opposite sides of the center square, cutting them to the required length.

3 Sew a Fabric 6 dark strip to the remaining two sides of the square, overlapping the first two light strips as shown.

4 Add a second round of light and dark strips, overlapping and cutting them to length as before.

5 Repeat for each round of the square until you have added five strips to each side, keeping the light and dark fabrics on opposite sides of the block.

A

Cut 1 of Fabric 11

B

Cut 1 each of Fabrics 1–10

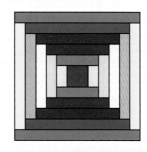

Variations

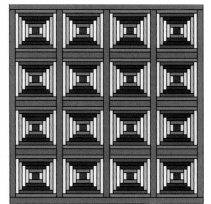

Blocks set with sashings and a plain border in a dark color.

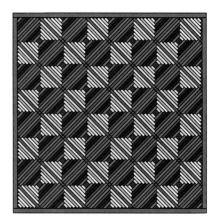

Blocks set on point with sashings, border, and posts.

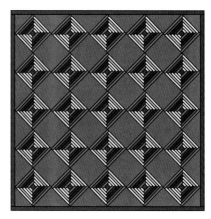

Blocks set on point with alternate plain squares and triangles.

Orange Peel

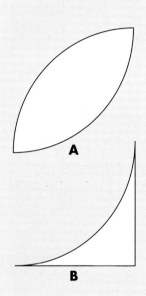

TEMPLATES ▾

A

B

Although published under this name only since 1898, this is actually a very old pattern also known as Melon Patch and Lafayette. For such a simple idea, it produces some very impressive patterns. It is an easy block to piece because the gentle curves present no problems, but you could make it even easier by appliquéing the A patches onto squares of fabric. The quilt is finished with a mitered border.

FABRICS ▾

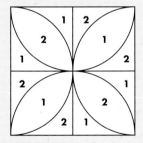

1 *DARK*
2 *LIGHT*

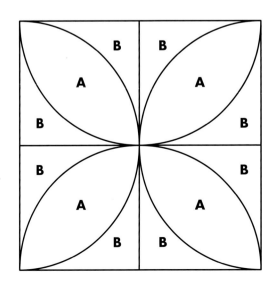

Drafting

Enlarge the block diagram to the required size and make templates.

Make a quick sketch of the block and pin scraps of your fabrics to it to use as reference.

Making the block

✂

1 Cut out all the fabric in the required shapes as directed.

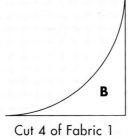

Cut 2 of Fabric 1
Cut 2 of Fabric 2

Cut 4 of Fabric 1
Cut 4 of Fabric 2

2 Join two Fabric 1 B patches to each Fabric 2 A patch.

 × 2

3 Join two Fabric 2 B patches to each Fabric 1 A patch.

 × 2

4 Join the pieced units in pairs.

5 Join the pairs to complete the block.

Variations

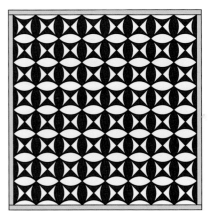

Blocks set on point with a plain border.

Blocks set on point with sashings, border, and posts.

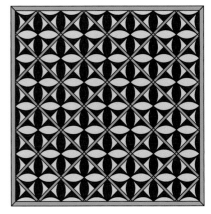

The blue fabric has been replaced with beige and the blocks set on point with narrow green sashings and posts and a wider mitered border.

SKILL LEVEL ▾

TEMPLATES ▾

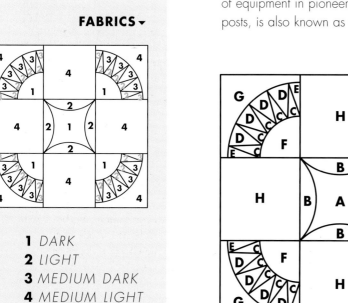

A

B

C

D   E

F

G

H

FABRICS ▾

1 DARK
2 LIGHT
3 MEDIUM DARK
4 MEDIUM LIGHT

Circular Saw

This is an old-time pattern, the name of which, like so many traditional patterns, reflects the surroundings of the women who made them—no doubt saws were important pieces of equipment in pioneer times. The pattern, finished here with a border and corner posts, is also known as Oriole Window and Four Little Fans.

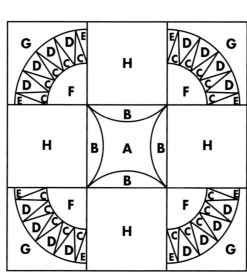

Drafting

Enlarge the block diagram to the required size and make templates.

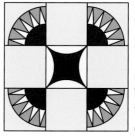

Make a quick sketch of the block and pin scraps of your fabrics to it to use as reference.

Making the block

✂

1 Cut out all the fabric in the required shapes as directed.

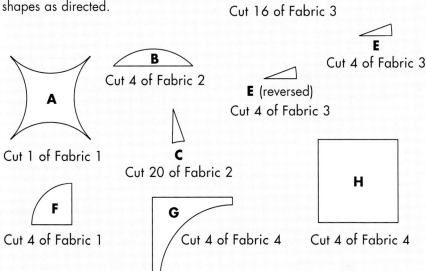

D
Cut 16 of Fabric 3

E
Cut 4 of Fabric 3

E (reversed)
Cut 4 of Fabric 3

B
Cut 4 of Fabric 2

A
Cut 1 of Fabric 1

C
Cut 20 of Fabric 2

F
Cut 4 of Fabric 1

G
Cut 4 of Fabric 4

H
Cut 4 of Fabric 4

2 Piece five C patches and four D patches together, then add an E and reversed E patch at each end.

 × 4

3 Add an F and G patch to complete the corner units.

 × 4

4 Sew a B patch to each side of Patch A to make the center square.

5 Join the pieced units and H patches in rows, then join the rows to complete the block.

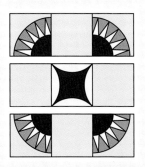

Variations

Blocks set on point with a plain border.

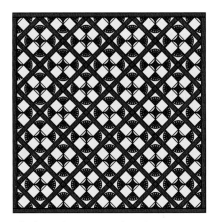

Blocks set on point with sashings and posts and a plain border.

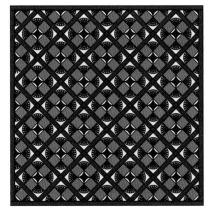

The same setting is used here, but this time the H patches are made from dark rather than light fabric, which emphasizes the double grid effect.

Suspension Bridge

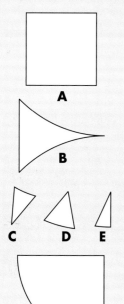

A
B
C D E
F

FABRICS ▾

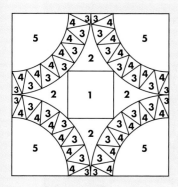

1 *MEDIUM*
2 *DARK*
3 *MEDIUM LIGHT*
4 *LIGHT*
5 *MEDIUM DARK*

Published as Suspension Bridge by the Ladies Art Company, this block was known traditionally as Sunflower or Indian Summer. You will see that when blocks are repeated, Sunflower is an appropriate name. Blocks with curves are more challenging to piece but are well worth the effort, and you can always choose to piece them by hand to make life easy. This quilt is finished with a plain border.

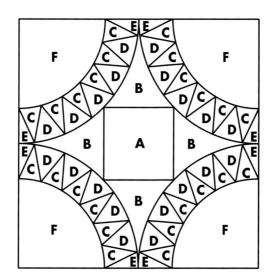

Drafting

Enlarge the block diagram to the required size and make templates.

Make a quick sketch of the block and pin scraps of your fabrics to it to use as reference.

Making the block

✂

1 Cut out all the fabric in the required shapes as directed.

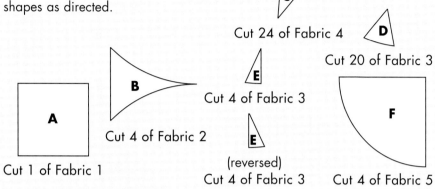

Cut 24 of Fabric 4

A Cut 1 of Fabric 1

B Cut 4 of Fabric 2

C Cut 24 of Fabric 4

E Cut 4 of Fabric 3

E (reversed) Cut 4 of Fabric 3

D Cut 20 of Fabric 3

F Cut 4 of Fabric 5

2 Piece a B patch to each side of Patch A to form the center of the block.

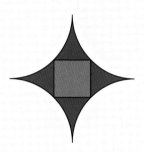

3 Piece six C patches and five D patches together, then add an E and reversed E patch at each end.

 × 4

4 Join a pieced arc to each side of the center unit.

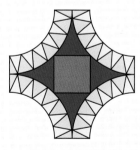

5 Join an F patch at each corner to complete the block.

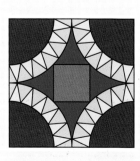

Variations

Blocks set on point with sashings, posts, and a plain border.

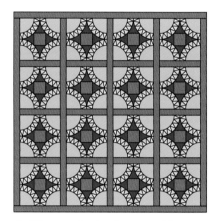

A different color has been used for the F patches here, and the blocks are set straight with sashings and a plain border.

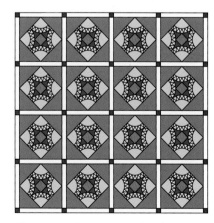

The same color variation, but this time the blocks are set on point with a plain triangle added to each side, then set with sashings, border, and posts.

Mill Wheel

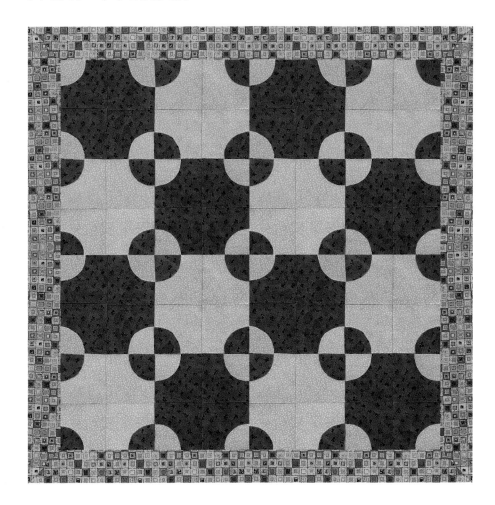

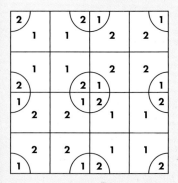
This traditional pattern is also known as Steeplechase, perhaps because it resembles the designs on jockeys' caps. The block is developed from two simple units and makes a delightful scrap quilt if enough contrast is maintained between the fabrics. This quilt is finished with a mitered border. As with many blocks with curves, you can piece curved patches together as described here or sew the B patches onto squares of fabric.

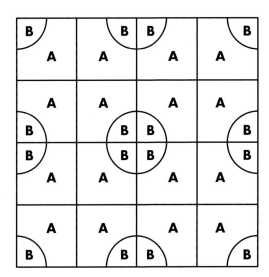

Drafting

Enlarge the block diagram to the required size and make templates.

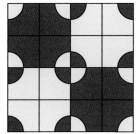

Make a quick sketch of the block and pin scraps of your fabrics to it to use as reference.

Making the block

✂

1 Cut out all the fabric in the required shapes as directed.

A

Cut 8 of Fabric 1
Cut 8 of Fabric 2

B

Cut 8 of Fabric 1
Cut 8 of Fabric 2

2 Piece Fabric 1 A patches and Fabric 2 B patches together.

 × 8

3 Piece Fabric 2 A patches and Fabric 1 B patches together.

 × 8

4 Join four units of each color group together.

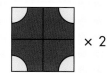 × 2

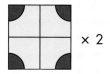 × 2

5 Join the pieced units in pairs, then join the pairs to complete the block.

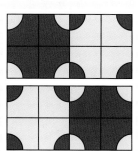

Variations

Blocks set on point with narrow sashings and posts and a wider border and posts.

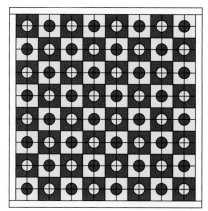

Rotating the pieced patches in each of the four squares of the block creates a new block known as Polka Dot.

Polka Dot blocks set with wide sashings, border, and posts.

Pincushion

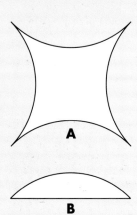

A

B

This block gains its effect from the contrasting colors used in the positive/negative placement of the shapes. It works well if you use strong light/dark contrast between the two fabrics. As with many blocks involving curved shapes, you can construct it either by piecing or by appliquéing the B patches onto squares of fabric. This example is finished with a plain border.

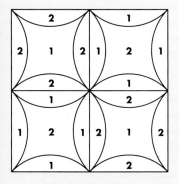

1 *LIGHT*
2 *DARK*

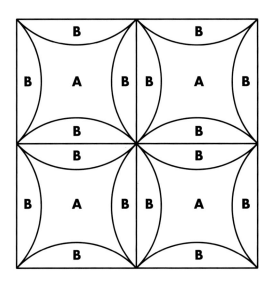

Drafting

Enlarge the block diagram to the required size and make templates.

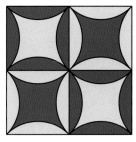

Make a quick sketch of the block and pin scraps of your fabrics to it to use as reference.

Making the block

1 Cut out all the fabric in the required shapes as directed.

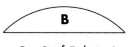

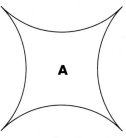

B
Cut 8 of Fabric 1
Cut 8 of Fabric 2

A
Cut 2 of Fabric 1
Cut 2 of Fabric 2

2 Sew a Fabric 2 B patch to each side of the Fabric 1 A patches.

 × 2

3 Join a Fabric 1 B patch to each side of the Fabric 2 A patches.

 × 2

4 Joined the pieced units in pairs.

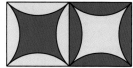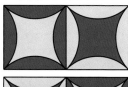

5 Join the pairs to complete the block.

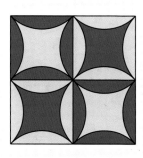

Variations

Blocks set with wide sashings and posts and a plain border.

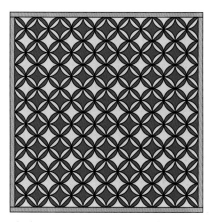

Blocks set on point create an all-over pattern of light and dark diamonds and circles.

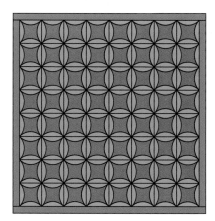

Instead of alternating the light and dark colors in each corner unit of the block, here all of the A patches are red and all of the B patches are green.

Hands All Around

TEMPLATES ▾

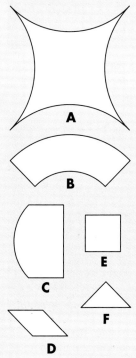

A

B

C

E

F

D

FABRICS ▾

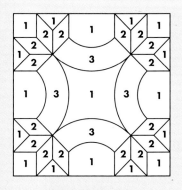

1 *MEDIUM*
2 *LIGHT*
3 *DARK*

Hands All Around was a dance figure in pioneer days in the Midwest. The piecing needs care but the delightful secondary patterns that appear when blocks are repeated make the effort well worthwhile. You can piece it completely or sew the B and D patches onto a large background square of Fabric 1. This quilt is finished with a mitered border.

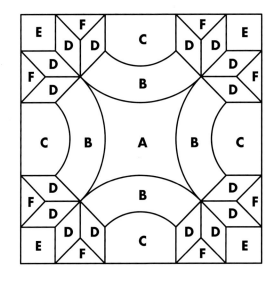

Drafting

Enlarge the block diagram to the required size and make templates.

Make a quick sketch of the block and pin scraps of your fabrics to it to use as reference.

Making the block

✂

1 Cut out all the fabric in the required shapes as directed.

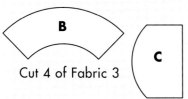

Cut 16 of Fabric 2

Cut 4 of Fabric 3

Cut 4 of Fabric 1

Cut 4 of Fabric 1

Cut 8 of Fabric 1

Cut 1 of Fabric 1

2 Join a B patch to each side of Patch A to form the center of the block.

3 Add a C patch to each curved edge.

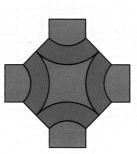

4 Piece groups of four D patches together, then add them to each corner of the center unit, setting in the seams (see page 27).

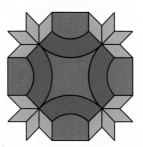

5 Set in the E and F patches around the edges to complete the block.

Variations

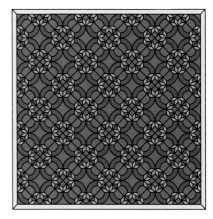

Blocks set on point with half and quarter blocks around the edges and a mitered border.

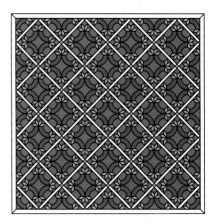

Blocks set on point with sashings and posts and a mitered border.

Blocks set on point with a plain triangle added to each side, then set with sashings, posts, and a mitered border.

SKILL LEVEL ▾

TEMPLATES ▾

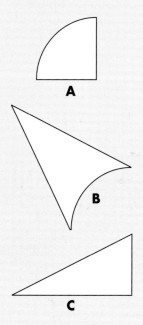

A

B

C

FABRICS ▾

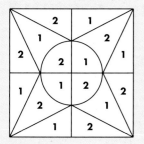

1 *LIGHT*
2 *DARK*

Compass Quilt

This simple block, finished here with a mitered border, produces stunning graphic effects. It is important to sew the corner triangles accurately so that you get sharp points where they meet between blocks. Cut the C patches so that the straight grain of the fabric is on the outside; otherwise, the edges may stretch and distort the measurements. To make things easier, you could sew B patches onto squares of fabric.

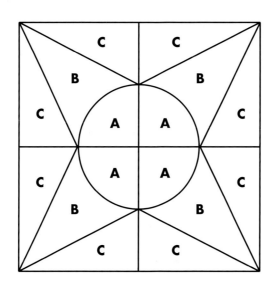

Drafting

Enlarge the block diagram to the required size and make templates.

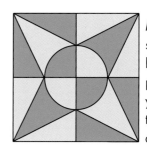

Make a quick sketch of the block and pin scraps of your fabrics to it to use as reference.

Making the block

1 Cut out all the fabric in the required shapes as directed.

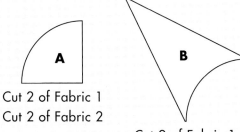
A
Cut 2 of Fabric 1
Cut 2 of Fabric 2

B
Cut 2 of Fabric 1
Cut 2 of Fabric 2

C
Cut 2 of Fabric 1
Cut 2 of Fabric 2

C (reversed)
Cut 2 of Fabric 1
Cut 2 of Fabric 2

2 Piece the A and B patches together in alternate colors.

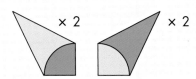

3 Add a C and reversed C patch to each pieced unit.

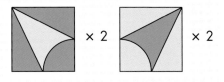

4 Join the pieced units in pairs.

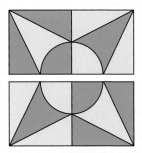

5 Join the pairs to complete the block.

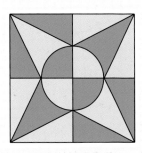

Variations

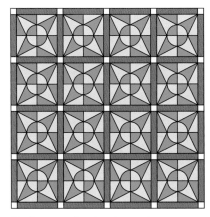

Blocks set with a border, sashings, and posts.

Blocks set on point with half and quarter blocks around the edges and finished with a border, sashings, and posts.

The green fabric has been replaced with dark gray for a more dramatic effect. Although the blocks are set on point with sashings and posts like the previous example, the different placement of the blocks avoids the use of quarter blocks in each corner.

Bleeding Hearts

SKILL LEVEL ▾

TEMPLATES ▾

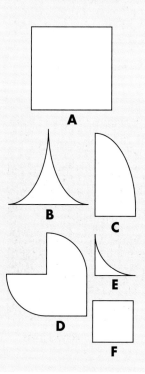

A

B

C

E

D

F

FABRICS ▾

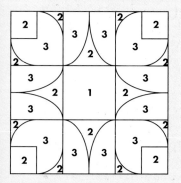

1 *MEDIUM*
2 *LIGHT*
3 *DARK*

This block, finished here with a plain border, looks more complex than it actually is. It is constructed from two different pieced units and a center square; provided you cut the patches with accurate seam allowances, the piecing should not present any problems. If you prefer, however, you could appliqué the C and D patches onto a background square; Patch A can be pieced into or sewn onto the background.

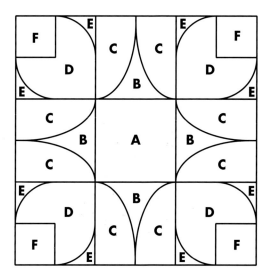

Drafting

Enlarge the block diagram to the required size and make templates.

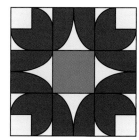

Make a quick sketch of the block and pin scraps of your fabrics to it to use as reference.

Making the block

✂

1 Cut out all the fabric in the required shapes as directed.

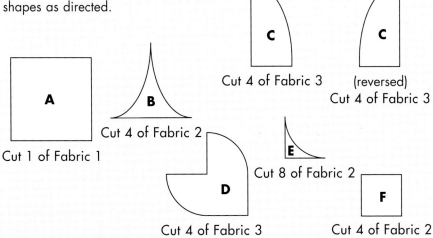

Cut 1 of Fabric 1

Cut 4 of Fabric 2

C
Cut 4 of Fabric 3

C (reversed)
Cut 4 of Fabric 3

E
Cut 8 of Fabric 2

D
Cut 4 of Fabric 3

F
Cut 4 of Fabric 2

2 Join a C and reversed C patch to each B patch to form the side units.

 × 4

3 Join an E patch to each curved edge of the D patches.

 × 4

4 Add an F patch to complete the corner units, setting in the seams (see page 27).

 × 4

5 Join the pieced units and A patch in rows, then join the rows to complete the block.

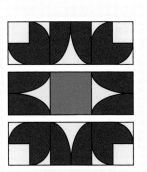

Variations

Blocks set with sashings, border, and posts.

Blocks set on point with monochrome border, sashings, and posts.

Blocks set on point with a plain triangle added to each side, then finished with a mitered border and sashings made from Fabric 3.

Grandmother's Fan

SKILL LEVEL ▾

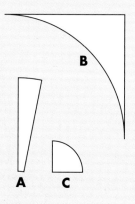

TEMPLATES ▾

B

A   C

FABRICS ▾

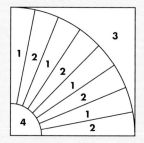

1 *MEDIUM LIGHT*
2 *MEDIUM DARK*
3 *LIGHT*
4 *DARK*

Grandmother's Fan is a very old pattern that probably has its origins in a time when no well-dressed lady's outfit was complete without a fan. It can be made with any number of scrap fabrics and will always look effective. You can piece the whole block from patches, or appliqué the fan—either pieced together first or patch by patch—onto a background square. This example is finished with a mitered border.

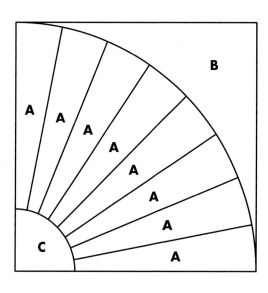

Drafting

Enlarge the block diagram to the required size and make templates.

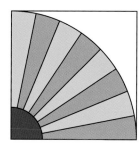

Make a quick sketch of the block and pin scraps of your fabrics to it to use as reference.

Making the block

1 Cut out all the fabric in the required shapes as directed.

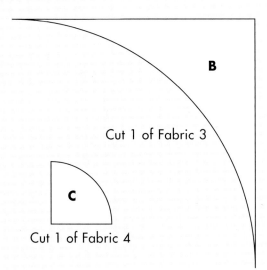

B

Cut 1 of Fabric 3

C

Cut 1 of Fabric 4

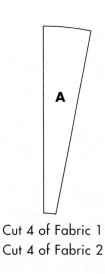

A

Cut 4 of Fabric 1
Cut 4 of Fabric 2

2 Piece the A patches together, alternating the colors, to form the fan blades.

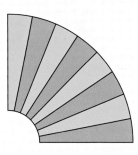

3 Add Patch C at the base of the fan blades.

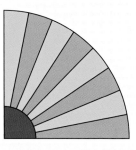

4 Join Patch B to complete the block.

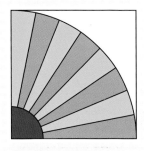

Variations

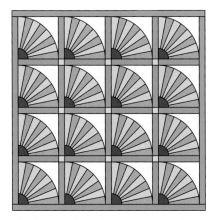

Blocks set with sashings, posts, and a plain border.

Blocks set on point with sashings, posts, and a plain border.

Blocks rotated to form circles and set with narrow sashings.

Japanese Fan

SKILL LEVEL ▾

TEMPLATES ▾

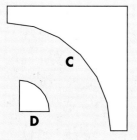

A   **B**

C

D

FABRICS ▾

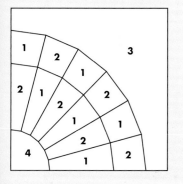

1 *DARK*
2 *MEDIUM LIGHT*
3 *MEDIUM DARK*
4 *LIGHT*

An eye-catching variation on the fan theme, the Japanese Fan dates from the 1930s when there was a vogue for all things Japanese. This is another block that can either be pieced completely or by appliquéing the pieced fan onto a square of background fabric. This quilt is finished with a border and corner posts.

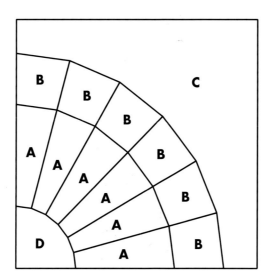

Drafting

Enlarge the block diagram to the required size and make templates.

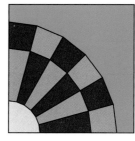

Make a quick sketch of the block and pin scraps of your fabrics to it to use as reference.

Making the block

✂

1 Cut out all the fabric in the required shapes as directed.

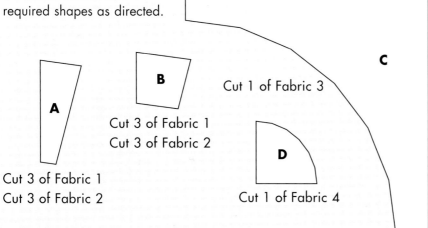

A

Cut 3 of Fabric 1
Cut 3 of Fabric 2

B

Cut 3 of Fabric 1
Cut 3 of Fabric 2

C

Cut 1 of Fabric 3

D

Cut 1 of Fabric 4

2 Piece pairs of contrasting colored A and B patches together to make the fan blades.

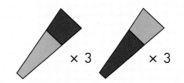

× 3   × 3

3 Join the blades together, alternating the colors.

4 Join Patch D at the base of the fan blades.

5 Add Patch C to complete the block.

Variations

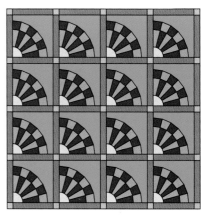

Blocks set with sashings, border, and posts.

Blocks set on point with narrow sashings and posts and a wider plain border.

Blocks in a different color combination rotated to form circles and set with sashings, border, and posts.

Snake Trail

SKILL LEVEL ⏷

TEMPLATES ⏷

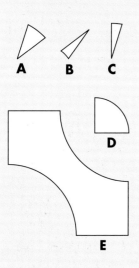

A   B   C

D

E

The evocatively named Snake Trail has also been published as Rattlesnake and Rocky Road Around California. This example is finished with a mitered border. The block is made from two fans placed in opposite corners of a square, so you can make it by piecing just the fan components and appliquéing them onto a background square or by piecing the whole block.

FABRICS ⏷

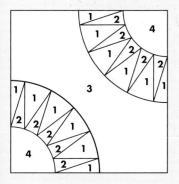

1 LIGHT
2 MEDIUM
3 MEDIUM DARK
4 DARK

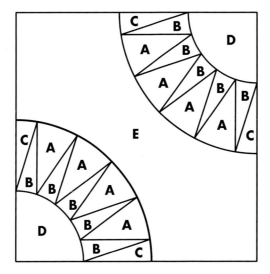

Drafting

Enlarge the block diagram to the required size and make templates.

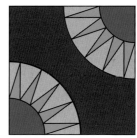

Make a quick sketch of the block and pin scraps of your fabrics to it to use as reference.

Making the block

✂

1 Cut out all the fabric in the required shapes as directed.

A
Cut 8 of Fabric 1

B
Cut 10 of Fabric 2

C
Cut 2 of Fabric 1

C
(reversed)
Cut 2 of Fabric 1

D
Cut 2 of Fabric 4

E
Cut 1 of Fabric 3

2 Piece four A and five B patches together.

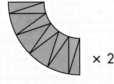 × 2

3 Join a C and reversed C patch to opposite ends of the pieced units to form the fan blades.

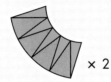 × 2

4 Add a D patch to complete each fan.

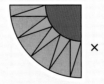 × 2

5 Join the fans to opposite sides of Patch E to complete the block.

Variations

Blocks rotated to form a concentric pattern.

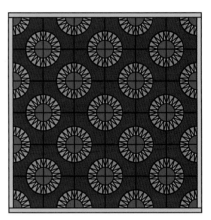

Alternate blocks rotated to form a Sun design.

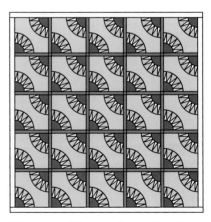

Blocks in a different color combination set with contrasting narrow sashings and posts and a wider plain border.

SKILL LEVEL ▾

TEMPLATES ▾

A

B

C　　D

FABRICS ▾

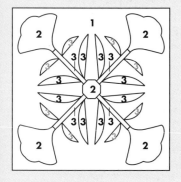

1 *LIGHT*
2 *DARK*
3 *MEDIUM*

Peonies

If you have not tried appliqué before, this traditional favorite is the perfect block on which to learn and practice the basic techniques. This example is finished with a mitered border. Although the flower heads are made from a single shape, it is easy to add embellishment by embroidering lines to distinguish the individual petals, although they look equally good without embellishment.

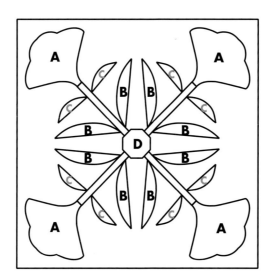

Drafting

Enlarge the block diagram to the required size and make templates.

Make a quick sketch of the block and pin scraps of your fabrics to it to use as reference.

Making the block

✄

1 Cut out a background square of Fabric 1 at the size of the finished block, plus a seam allowance. Cut the remaining fabric in the required shapes as directed, reserving some Fabric 3 for the stems.

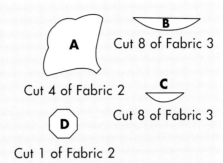

A — Cut 4 of Fabric 2

B — Cut 8 of Fabric 3

C — Cut 8 of Fabric 3

D — Cut 1 of Fabric 2

2 Transfer the block diagram onto the background square (see page 32).

3 Make bias strips for the stems from Fabric 3 (see page 33). Pin the stems over the drawn guidelines, then sew them in place.

4 Pin or press the B and C patches to the background square, then sew them in place.

5 Apply and sew the A and D patches to the background square to complete the block.

Variations

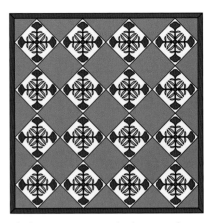

Blocks set on point with alternate plain squares. Plain triangles around the edges and a mitered border complete the quilt.

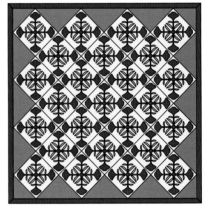

25 blocks set on point, with plain triangles around the edges.

Alternate blocks have been appliquéd onto light and dark background squares. The blocks are set with sashings and a mitered border.

Rose of Sharon

SKILL LEVEL ▾

TEMPLATES ▾

A

B

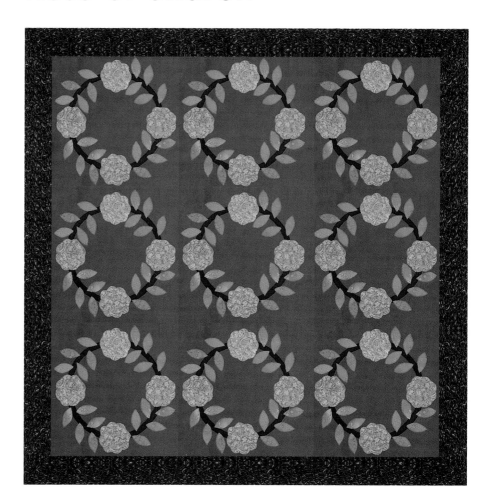

Wreaths make beautiful appliqué blocks, and some are very complex. This is one of the easier designs, but the circular stem onto which the flowers and petals are appliquéd needs care. Use a compass to draw a double circle on the background square so that you get an accurate shape without the need for a template. This quilt is finished with a mitered border.

FABRICS ▾

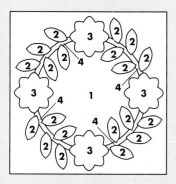

1 *MEDIUM*
2 *MEDIUM LIGHT*
3 *LIGHT*
4 *DARK*

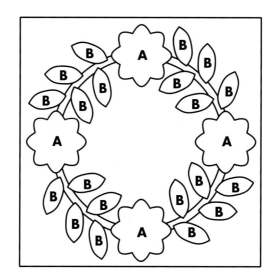

Drafting

Enlarge the block diagram to the required size and make templates.

Make a quick sketch of the block and pin scraps of your fabrics to it to use as reference.

Making the block

1 Cut out a background square of Fabric 1 at the size of the finished block, plus a seam allowance. Cut Fabrics 2 and 3 in the required shapes as directed.

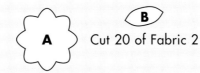
A

B Cut 20 of Fabric 2

Cut 4 of Fabric 3

2 Press the background square to create creases both horizontally and diagonally, then use a compass to draw a double circle for the stem. The outer circle should bisect the diagonal lines about midway from the center point; the inner circle should be ½ inch (1.3 cm) inside this.

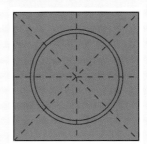

3 Make bias strips for the stem from Fabric 4 (see page 33). Pin the bias strips to the background square, easing them around the marked circle, then sew them in place.

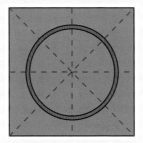

4 Pin or press the A patches to the background square, then sew them in place. You can press out the creases after this stage if you wish.

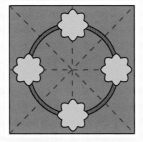

5 Apply and sew the B patches to the stem to complete the block.

Variations

Blocks set on point with plain triangles around the edges and finished with sashings, posts, and a mitered border.

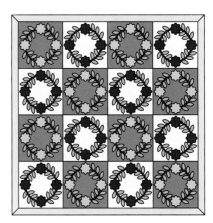

Different colors have been used for the flowers and background squares of alternate blocks.

Alternate blocks in different color combinations set with sashings and a mitered border.

Oak Leaf Wreath

SKILL LEVEL ▾

TEMPLATES ▾

A

B

C

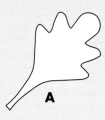

This is a very early appliqué pattern, thought to date from the 1820s. It is traditionally worked in red and green on a plain background. Blocks of this sort intended for use in bed quilts were often worked on a larger than average scale, such as 14 inches (35 cm) rather than the conventional 12 inches (30 cm). However, you can choose to scale it up or down to whatever size you wish. This example has a mitered border.

FABRICS ▾

1 *LIGHT*
2 *DARK*
3 *MEDIUM*

Drafting

Enlarge the block diagram to the required size and make templates.

Make a quick sketch of the block and pin scraps of your fabrics to it to use as reference.

Making the block

1 Cut out a background square of Fabric 1 at the size of the finished block, plus a seam allowance. Cut the remaining fabric in the required shapes as directed.

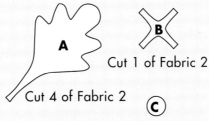

A
Cut 4 of Fabric 2

B
Cut 1 of Fabric 2

C
Cut 12 of Fabric 3

2 Transfer the block diagram onto the background square (see page 32).

3 Pin or press Patch B to the center of the square, then sew it in place.

4 Apply and sew the A patches in place.

5 Apply and sew the C patches to the background square to complete the block.

Variations

Blocks set with sashings, border, and posts.

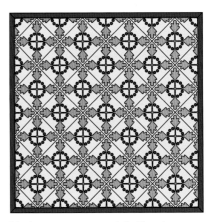

Blocks set on point with half and quarter blocks around the edges and a mitered border.

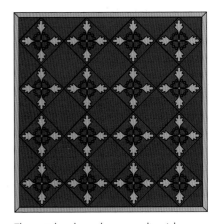

The patches have been appliquéd to a dark background square to create a more contemporary and dramatic effect. The blocks are set on point and alternated with plain squares and triangles.

Triple Flower

SKILL LEVEL ▾

TEMPLATES ▾

A

B

C

FABRICS ▾

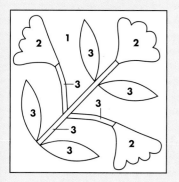

1 *LIGHT*
2 *MEDIUM*
3 *DARK*

This appliqué quilt, finished here with a border and corner posts, is a typical folk art design. The diagonal slant of the pattern means that repeated blocks produce some interesting effects. Although each flower head is formed from a single patch, you can embellish the flowers in any way you like when the block is finished. You could also adjust the shapes of the leaves into more organic curves if you prefer.

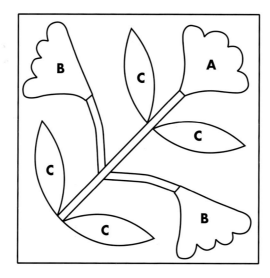

Drafting

Enlarge the block diagram to the required size and make templates.

Make a quick sketch of the block and pin scraps of your fabrics to it to use as reference.

Making the block

✂

1 Cut out a background square of Fabric 1 at the size of the finished block, plus a seam allowance. Cut the remaining fabric in the required shapes as directed, reserving some Fabric 3 for the stems.

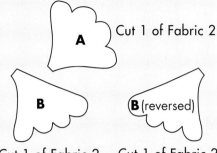

A — Cut 1 of Fabric 2

B

C — Cut 4 of Fabric 3

B — Cut 1 of Fabric 2

B (reversed) — Cut 1 of Fabric 2

2 Transfer the block diagram onto the background square (see page 32).

3 Make bias strips for the stems from Fabric 3 (see page 33). Pin the stems over the drawn guidelines, then sew them in place.

4 Pin or press the A, B, and reversed B patches to the background square, then sew them in place.

5 Apply and sew the C patches to the background square to complete the block.

Variations

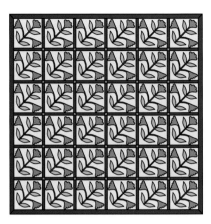

Blocks set with sashings and posts and a mitered border.

Blocks set on point with plain triangles around the edges. The posts and mitered border are in a contrasting color to the sashings.

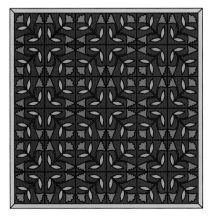

The patches have been appliquéd to a dark background square instead of a light one, and alternate blocks have been rotated to form a pattern of squares and circles.

Mexican Rose

SKILL LEVEL ▾

TEMPLATES ▾

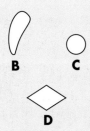

A

B   C

D

There are several appliqué patterns called Mexican Rose, this one dating from around 1842. It is unusual in combining geometric shapes with the organic shapes of the petals. Although the same template is used to make all the petals, slight variations would emphasize the organic design without diminishing the overall effect of the pattern. This quilt is finished with a mitered border.

FABRICS ▾

1 MEDIUM LIGHT
2 DARK
3 MEDIUM DARK
4 LIGHT
5 MEDIUM

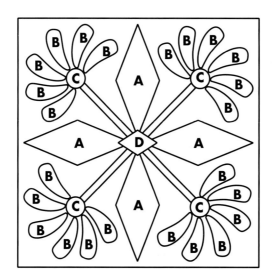

Drafting

Enlarge the block diagram to the required size and make templates.

Make a quick sketch of the block and pin scraps of your fabrics to it to use as reference.

Making the block

✄

1 Cut out a background square of Fabric 1 at the size of the finished block, plus a seam allowance. Cut Fabrics 2, 3, and 4 in the required shapes as directed.

A
Cut 4 of Fabric 2

B
Cut 12 of Fabric 2
Cut 12 of Fabric 3

D
Cut 1 of Fabric 3

C
Cut 4 of Fabric 4

2 Transfer the block diagram onto the background square (see page 32). Make bias strips for the stems from Fabric 5 (see page 33). Pin the stems over the drawn guidelines, then sew them in place.

3 Pin or press the B patches to the background square, alternating the colors of the petals, then sew them in place.

4 Apply and sew the A patches between the flowers.

5 Apply and sew the C patches to the center of each flower and the D patch to the center of the design to complete the block.

Variations

Blocks set on point without sashings create a pretty all-over floral quilt.

Blocks set with sashings and a mitered border in the same color.

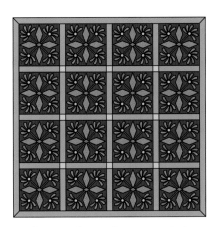

Appliquéing the patches onto a dark background fabric creates a bolder, less traditional-looking quilt.

Index